T0028669

"Alan Noble unveils the sheer paralyzing terror of a full-blown panic attack as well as just what chronic low-grade melancholy feels like inside. Some days it's all you can do just to get out of bed. Noble has no quick fixes to recommend. Rather, he points suffering Christians to the suffering Savior as the sole reason to keep on keeping on. In God's kingdom little things count: a cup of cold water given in Jesus' name, for instance. Alan Noble reminds us that simply doing the next thing can be a courageous act of faith—like getting out of bed when we'd rather not."

Harold L. Senkbeil, author of *Christ and Calamity: Grace and Gratitude in the Darkest Valley* and executive director emeritus of Doxology: The Lutheran Center for Spiritual Care and Counsel

"Alan Noble has given us another great gift in writing this short, honest, and deeply moving book on the powerful witness to the goodness of life and of God of simply getting out of bed each day, especially when we experience mental suffering or affliction. It contains many gems of wisdom and profound truth, such as living one day at a time, one step at a time, accepting God's love and grace and the help of others—including mental health professionals and lay people—and reaching out to others in community. Highly recommended!"

Siang-Yang Tan, professor of psychology at Fuller Theological Seminary and author of *Counseling and Psychotherapy: A Christian Perspective*

"Candid, convicting, and deeply honest. Alan Noble is unflinching in his portrayal of both the depths of despair and a bedrock belief in the irreducible value of the human life. He convinces us to see the simple, yet sometimes seemingly insurmountable, act of getting out of bed as an act of faith and a witness to the goodness of God beyond feeling or circumstance. I will recommend this book."

Diana Gruver, author of *Companions in the Darkness: Seven Saints Who Struggled with Depression and Doubt*

"In this inspiring and thought-provoking book, Alan Noble comes alongside us in our inevitable suffering, reminds us that it is part of the human condition, and compassionately challenges us to inhabit life as a gift from God."

Todd W. Hall, professor of psychology at Rosemead School of Psychology and author of *The Connected Life*

"In these wisdom-filled pages, Alan Noble explores how the courageous act of rising out of bed can be both a defiance of despair and a testimony to the goodness of God. With empathy borne out of personal experience and hope forged in affliction, Alan ponders the questions, Why live? and How, then, shall we live, especially in the midst of sorrow and suffering? Prepare to be enlarged and encouraged by his insights. *On Getting Out of Bed* is a sturdy, important book."

Sharon Garlough Brown, author of the Sensible Shoes series and the Shades of Light series

On
Getting
Out of
Bed

The Burden & Gift of Living

Alan Noble

An imprint of InterVarsity Press
Downers Grove, Illinois

InterVarsity Press
P.O. Box 1400 | Downers Grove, IL 60515-1426
ivpress.com | email@ivpress.com

©2023 by Alan Noble

All rights reserved. No part of this book may be reproduced in any form without written permission from InterVarsity Press.

InterVarsity Press® is the publishing division of InterVarsity Christian Fellowship/USA®. For more information, visit intervarsity.org.

Scripture quotations, unless otherwise noted, are from The Holy Bible, English Standard Version, copyright © 2001 by Crossway Bibles, a division of Good News Publishers. Used by permission. All rights reserved.

Published in association with the literary agent Don Gates of The Gates Group, www.the-gates-group.com.

While any stories in this book are true, some names and identifying information may have been changed to protect the privacy of individuals.

The publisher cannot verify the accuracy or functionality of website URLs used in this book beyond the date of publication.

Cover design and image composite: David Fassett
Interior design: Jeanna Wiggins

ISBN 978-1-5140-0443-2 (print) | ISBN 978-1-5140-0444-9 (digital)

Printed in the United States of America ∞

Library of Congress Cataloging-in-Publication Data
A catalog record for this book is available from the Library of Congress.

29 28 27 26 25 24 23 | 13 12 11 10 9 8 7 6 5 4 3 2 1

DEDICATED TO

Brittany, Eleanor, Quentin, and Frances

—a family that suffers and loves together.

AUTHOR'S NOTE

THE SUBJECT OF THIS BOOK is mental suffering, and its assumption is that everyone experiences mental suffering at one point or another. This includes diagnosed mental illnesses and disorders and undiagnosed or even undiagnosable anxieties, depressions, and burdens of life. It includes illnesses that have clear biological causes and ones that don't have any clear cause at all. It includes the suffering of those who would say they have a "serious problem" and those who would vehemently deny that they have a problem at all. It includes examples from specific mental disorders and general experiences of mental distress. Although my subject is broad, it is not intended to be all-encompassing. I won't try to describe the experience of every mental illness. But I do believe that what follows will resonate with most people who have endured mental affliction. Life is difficult, and we experience that difficulty in different ways and to varying extents, but we always experience it in our hearts and minds. That experience is the subject of this book.

In many ways my approach is described by the historian of science Anne Harrington in her book *Mind Fixers*. After tracing the successes and failures of modern psychiatry, Harrington advocates for an alternative approach:

> Psychiatry has at least one possible alternative. . . . It could decide to return to a less hierarchical understanding of its place in the mental health and medical systems; one that . . . would acknowledge that mental suffering is a larger category than mental illness, and that even disorders with a likely biological basis are not *just* medical, because the experience of all human beings, ill or otherwise, are shaped by their cultural, social, and familial circumstances.[1]

Harrington's recommendation for the future of psychiatry is based on an understanding of the basic human experience, one that I share and that forms the basis of *On Getting Out of Bed*:

> We should keep in mind one very basic fact. Among the very many people who present with a mental affliction, some are (almost certainly) suffering from a real illness, one that is understandable (in principle) like any other mental complaint. By the same token, others are (almost

certainly) not. Mental suffering takes many forms, only some of which have roots in disease. The suffering of those who are not really ill in any meaningful medical sense can still be acute.[2]

This book is for those who struggle with what Harrington calls "mental affliction." It is for their friends and family members. It is for pastors, teachers, and parents—to help them understand their loved one's suffering. It is for anyone who ever struggles to get out of bed.

I will not offer professional medical advice because I am not a medical professional. Neither will this be a memoir or a self-help book. In the spirit of Harrington's broad approach to addressing mental health, I'm going to share what I know. Take what you find to be true and helpful. Weigh it, pray about it, and discuss it with friends and loved ones. Some parts may not ring true to you, but they may describe the experience of your neighbor.

If you take away one truth, the one thing in this book I know with certainty, let it be this: your life is a good gift from a loving God, even when subjectively it doesn't feel good or like a gift, and even when you doubt that God is loving. Please get out of bed anyway.

What's the bravest thing you ever did? . . .
Getting up this morning.

CORMAC MCCARTHY, *THE ROAD*

I'VE KNOWN A LOT OF PEOPLE who have lived painful, tragic lives. When I was young, I assumed these people were abnormal. Their suffering was the exception that proved the rule that a well-lived life is a pleasant life.

People close to me went hungry and lived in filth. Some were addicted to alcohol, meth, cocaine, and God knows what else. They were willing to do almost anything to feel alive—even overdose. Others were orphaned, abandoned, neglected, and later imprisoned. Some were molested, raped, and beaten by parents, spouses, and family friends. They all lived hard, hard lives where their daily experiences were either acute suffering or prolonged numbness. And these horrors were passed down to their children and their grand-children. I don't know where it will end.

But as a child I assumed that these tragedies were outliers. I assumed that outside of my circle I would discover that most adults lived fairly pleasant and safe lives. Not perfect lives— not without difficulties and accidents—but generally pleasant, comfortable lives. A good job. A fulfilling marriage. An exciting sex life. A photogenic family. A sense of accomplishment. A new phone. Not too much debt. Reasonably good health. An abiding sense of happiness. Solidly middle class. Very Christian. A pleasant life. A normal life. A life I could have.

I didn't believe that I was owed this normal life. But my sense of the world and of Christianity was that if I put in the work and honored God with my time, none of these good things were out of reach. They were normal, reasonable expectations. It wasn't like I had grandiose visions of fame or riches. I just expected things to be nice if I took care of my business. And so I did.

As I grew older, my experiences mostly confirmed my expectations of what a normal life looked like. I met more people and they mostly seemed to be pretty happy. They would greet me with warm smiles and interesting conversations. They had nice things. They enjoyed themselves. Life came easy to them. Life was pleasant and safe.

The few people I met who had difficult lives seemed to choose their suffering. I could trace their problems back to a flaw in their character or intelligence. They also tended not to be Christians, or at least not *good* Christians. From what I could see, they had decided to be miserable or depressed or a failure or whatever. And I would think, *You know, if they just made better choices, if they were just disciplined and stopped making excuses, they wouldn't have to suffer this way.*

You can walk around for a long time thinking nonsense like this—that most adults have it together and live safe, pleasant lives, and that the ones who don't only have themselves to blame. It's easy to think like Job's friends.

∾

In fact, it's hard *not* to think like this, even when you grow up around tragedy and trauma, as I did. It's hard not to think like this because almost no one wants to tell you otherwise. There's a kind of unspoken conspiracy to ignore how difficult life is, or to reframe it as something romantic—a heroic challenge we overcome on our way to the good life. In this conspiracy we each try to hide our scars, even from those closest to us and sometimes even from ourselves. Almost every cultural institution, church, government, or corporation promises you a good life if you just do what they ask. Make the right life choices. Marry the right person. Go to the right church. Get the right education. Work the right job. Buy the right products. And you'll be fine.

Whatever challenges we face can be solved. That's society's promise. Whatever problem you have, someone has developed a method for overcoming it. A pill. A treatment. A mindset. Which means that if you *don't* overcome your problems, it's your own fault. You really should have tried harder. You should have shown more initiative. You should have chosen the right technique. Because the normal life is a pleasant life for those who merit it.

I believed all this, and I was wrong. The people close to me weren't anomalies, they were the norm. While not everyone will experience the kinds of trauma they did, suffering—even profound mental affliction and personal tragedy—is a normal part of human life. Sometimes the tragedy strikes us directly. Other times we experience it through those we love (suffering with others is its own kind of suffering, and it is no less real or significant for being indirect). One way or another, it gets us. Once I grew close to other adults, people who had seemed to "have their lives together," that's what I discovered. Life is far more difficult than we let on.

≈

Get to know someone really well, and almost without fail, you will discover a person who routinely struggles to get out of bed in the morning. And not just because they're tired.

8

They can't get out of bed because once they step foot on the floor, they will be launched into a day that is uncertain and lifeless and in some ways impossible.

Here are some things you will see if you get to know people: you'll discover someone who suffers panic attacks every time there's another mass shooting, someone who cannot stop obsessing over how they may have failed as a parent, someone who cannot eat or who cannot stop eating because of the guilt they feel from being sexually assaulted, someone with a nearly debilitating mental disorder that only manifested after they were married and had kids and now their spouse seriously considers divorce on an almost monthly basis, or someone who is stuck in the habit of living even though they feel terribly alone and bored. None of these scenarios are unusual.

Think about someone you know who is living the good life: someone well dressed, confident, smiling, high achieving, maybe even attractive and intelligent and funny. Nine times out of ten, they are carrying around something unspeakably painful. And often, when you learn *what* that pain is, it'll be something completely unexpected. You weren't even aware that people could suffer like that. Maybe you didn't know how helpless it can feel to have an adult sibling addicted to meth. Or to carry the guilt of learning that your child was abused at a sleepover. There are diseases and disorders and burdens you have never imagined, carried like boulders on the backs of the same people who smile and tell you that they are doing "good." Every time you ask them, "How's it going?" they'll say, "Good! I'm doing good. How about you?" Maybe they don't trust you, or they are terrified to vocalize their suffering. But maybe they just don't know *how* to say how bad they feel. So why should they even try?

Most of these people will show no obvious signs of the despair that follows them around, or at least those signs will be subtle and veiled. They might surface in a prayer request ("Can I just ask you guys to pray for a stressful situation at work?"), sudden moodiness, or distracting addictions like social media or porn or work. But mostly these people are high-functioning adults.

We may go through periods where we break down and stare blankly at our email inbox, or debate whether to get out of bed, or feel we can't physically move, but for the most part, we function. We get up. We eat. We work. We buy things. We are entertained. We are stimulated. We sleep. But the darkness is there, waiting for the right moment to re-assert itself. And it does. Unbidden and unwanted and too often unavoidable.

You may never experience long-term, intense depression or anxiety, but there will very likely be a period of your life when you feel something similar, as if you are a ghost haunting your own life.

Living in a society governed by *technique* conditions us to believe that in every way life is easier than it ever has been. Technique is the use of rational methods to maximize efficiency, and we see it everywhere: time-saving technology, apps that maximize our workouts, drugs that drown out our anxiety, ubiquitous entertainment in our pockets, and scientifically proven methods for parenting, working, eating, shopping, budgeting, folding clothes, sleeping, sex, dating, and buying a car.[3] The promise of technique is that we are collectively overcoming all the challenges to life through research, technology, and discipline. All you have to do is find the right self-help book or life hack or app or life coach or devotional.

But technique's promise that life is easier than ever turns out to be just another source of dread and shame: if life doesn't *have* to be this hard, if there are answers and methods and practices that can solve my problems, then it really *is* my fault that I'm overwhelmed or a failure. That's not to say that there aren't external forces that shape our lives: a corrupt political system can disadvantage us, we all have character flaws, and some people have a genetic advantage. But we have methods for overcoming these obstacles. There's always another technique I can use to fight a corrupt political system, improve my character, and compensate for my biology. So if I'm not living to my full potential, I'm to blame for not taking advantage of these methods.

This is one reason why we don't want to be honest when someone asks us how we are doing. Why admit to failure or weakness? If we tell the truth, they'll start offering advice, recommending some new method for "fixing" our problem, for overcoming anxiety or achieving our fullest potential or whatever. By the time they are done, we'll just feel the weight of a new obligation, another method to try, and another chance to fail. "Have you tried this diet?" "I heard regular exercise can improve your mental health. Maybe that's your problem." "Here's a book on prayer." "I heard this scientist on a podcast talk about how your mental disorder can actually be treated by drinking more water."

If you suffer from a chronic mental illness, these conversations can be particularly humiliating because they remind you of all the things that have already failed to cure you. And you just feel tired of the whole thing.

On top of the unmanageable burden technique places on our lives, our society is hypercompetitive. Everyone is vying for attention and validation. Publicly announcing your suffering, whether formally diagnosed or not, can be a real liability. While there is less stigma associated with things like mental illness than in the past, competing in the job market (or the marriage "market" or whatever) is hard enough without publicizing your weakness.

But what if our contemporary society is not actually built for *us*, for humans as God designed us? If that is the case, then *some*times anxiety and depression will be rational and moral responses to a fundamentally disordered environment. As I have argued in my book *You Are Not Your Own*, this is precisely the kind of society in which we find ourselves.[4]

Understanding the source of our modern dis-ease can help us resist it and work for a more human society. If I didn't believe that, I wouldn't have written a book on the subject. But however you *explain* the difficulty of living in the modern world, whatever theory you accept, you're still stuck with the reality that a normal life includes a great deal of suffering. Ultimately, you must have some reason to put up with such a life, some reason for still getting out of bed even when you know it will mean pain. Even though getting out of bed in the morning can be incredibly hard.

∼

Throughout our lives, the choice to get out of bed will weigh on us to different extents. Some days life feels effortless and we ride the momentum of our busy schedules. The alarm wakes us up and we don't stop or even slow down until we return to bed at night, feeling full and satisfied. But other days it feels impossible to get up. Like a boulder—or a regret or an uncertainty or some personal inadequacy—is sitting on our chest, compressing our lungs and pinning us to the bed. Like Gregor Samsa, the protagonist who wakes up as a bug in Franz Kafka's *Metamorphosis*, we sometimes think that if we just stay in bed and go back to sleep, we won't have to face our depression, anxiety, suffering, or fears.[5] Everyone has thoughts like this at some point. Don't let anyone tell you otherwise.

We have many terms for the different types of mental affliction that humans experience: depression, anxiety, clinical depression, melancholy, despair, low self-esteem, trauma, lethargy, boredom, guilt, lack of ambition, laziness, mourning, a failure to launch, exhaustion, burnout, mental illness, mental disorder, and so on. We have a massive medical field devoted to treating the problem through medication and therapy. We have a million self-help books and life coaches and social media mindset influencers to inspire us. But here's the thing: each morning it's you. Each morning *you* must choose to get out of bed or not. All the medication and cognitive therapy and latest research and self-care in the world can't replace your choice. This decision can be aided by these resources but never replaced by them. Which means that you have to have an answer to a fundamental question: Why get out of bed? Or, more bluntly, why live?

At root, these are the same questions because there are many ways to throw a life away, and most of them involve continuing to live. We like to think of suicide as a singular act: intentionally ending your life. But you can also destroy your life slowly through alcoholism and drug addiction. You can destroy your life through an addiction to gambling. You can destroy your life (and the lives of others) through abuse and violence. You can destroy your life passively by being so overcome with fear of failure that you cannot move. You can even destroy your life by giving up all hope and devoting yourself to fleeting, vacuous, mind-numbing pleasures. So this question is not primarily about what we normally think of as suicide. It includes that, but it also includes all the various ways we can deny the goodness of life and act in defiance of it—all the ways we can choose not to get out of bed and face the day.

Maybe this seems like a dumb or morose question to you. "Of course you should get out of bed! There's so much to do, so many beautiful things to experience! You'd have to be sick to even ask the question."

But it's not dumb at all. It's the most essential question in life. And it's not morose. What's morose is pretending that none of this matters. And the thing is, you must have an answer ready because you don't know when you'll need it, and when you need it, you won't have the time, energy, or willpower to go looking for answers. "When the time comes there will be no time."[6]

It's a straightforward question, but it's easy to ignore until one day it's all you can think about. Like so many other uncomfortable aspects of modern life, we are well adapted to distracting ourselves from the question of life's worth.

For some people this looks like a frantically busy life. As long as you're moving and doing, becoming the best version of yourself, it doesn't feel necessary to know *why* life is worth living. You're too busy living to question living.

For others, the perpetual hope of future pleasure keeps this question at bay. Yes, we all suffer in life, but the modern world is filled with pleasures. There's always something new to do, experience, or buy. Any time you feel bored or distressed, you can watch previews for a new TV series. You can try a new kind of ice cream. You can find some new kind of porn or someone new to sleep with. You can watch an Apple press conference or the NFL draft. When life feels unbearable, just remember something cool is just around the corner.

When we must finally face the question of life, many people turn to platitudes. We reassure one another that our lives are precious because life is precious. Or that the world needs us. Or that we each matter. So have hope!

Which is all fine and good until you actually think about it and realize that each of these phrases is an empty affirmation, a tautology. And then it starts to look a whole lot like we've been conditioned to lie to each other that life is worth living because we can't or won't accept the possibility that it's not. There's that unspoken conspiracy again.

In addition to busyness, pleasure, and platitudes, there is still one more way of avoiding this question: We can see the question itself, or the suffering that raises the question, as a sign of a treatable medical condition. If we can just treat the *illness*, the question won't matter anymore.

My mind's not right.

Robert Lowell, "Skunk Hour"

W E DON'T KNOW WHAT WE ARE DOING, and I think this is especially true about the way our society deals with mental health. In just the past fifteen years, I have witnessed a massive shift in how evangelicals—and Americans in general—understand mental health, and for the most part this has been a very good thing. Mental health has lost so much of its social stigma that it's not uncommon for some people to post frank confessions about their depression, anxiety, or PTSD on social media. Prescription psychotropic drug use is, at least officially, treated as normal and healthy and nothing to hide. To a limited extent, society has begun to see mental disorders like other diseases or ailments. They are things that happen *to* us. They aren't the result of weak character, sin, or laziness.

But I also suspect that for the vast majority of people, despair, trauma, sorrow, and mental illness remain hidden. Oh yes, *some* people are talking about mental health openly. Some even turn it into a brand. But the day-to-day experience of adult life has not changed much. "We each suffer our own ghosts," and mostly alone.[7] So even as we see greater attention paid to mental health and more emphasis placed on self-care, we still have a long way to go before we have a healthy and humane social understanding of mental illness and affliction.

There is a danger, however, in relying too heavily on the language of mental health. My concern is that our expectations of psychological treatments are not realistic. We hope that a diagnosis will provide concrete, specific answers. The unknown is much more frightening than the known, so it can be a great relief to receive a diagnosis. *If there's a diagnosis*, we think, *there must be a cure. This problem, like all other problems, can be fixed if I just take the right steps and find the correct technique.* But if you've ever been to counseling for an extended period or been medically treated for a disorder, you know that concrete answers are few and far between.

I'm not saying that psychology and psychiatry are dangerous secular practices and that you just need to pray harder. There is great value in both of these fields, and I have personally benefited from them. I am not opposed to counseling or medication: I regularly recommend both therapy and psychiatry to those I love, and I have witnessed profound improvements in some people who sought help. (This is the place where I'm supposed to share my psychological history to establish my credibility—but I'm not going to do that. My burdens are neither private nor public. Those who know, know. But that's beside the point. This isn't about me.)

The best mental health professionals are not scientists who offer precise, empirically objective diagnoses but students of the human heart and soul. They do not provide a taxonomy and rational explanation for your suffering but intuit with wisdom and compassion. They attend to you personally. By grace they may sketch out the contours of your suffering, but sometimes little more than that. They offer a sympathetic ear, wise advice, and ameliorating treatments, but only rarely something like a medical cure.

Psychiatrists can sometimes prescribe a medication that helps lessen your suffering, but disturbingly, we aren't sure *how* or *why* many popular antidepressants work.[8] And some drugs seem to have a higher likelihood of producing awful side effects than doing the one thing they are supposed to do. What we do know is that some medications work effectively for some people sometimes, and we know that untreated depression and anxiety can be deadly.

We desperately want mental illnesses to be as objectively diagnosable, measurable, and treatable as something like diabetes. This is what I mean by expectations. When explaining how mental illnesses are *real*, people will sometimes say something like, "You would never shame someone for having cancer or ascribe their disease to bad character. So why would you shame someone for having a mental illness?"

Except that sometimes people really do make bad health choices that lead to disease. And sometimes the symptoms of a mental illness can be worsened by our choices. While brain scans can show us signs of some mental illnesses, we can't get a depression biopsy or have our anxiety levels measured in our blood. It's all so uncertain. Which is frustrating because when you suffer from a mental illness, one of the things you want is some kind of certainty, something sure you can hold on to.

We don't even know what something as common as depression *is*. Not only have the definition, terminology, symptoms, treatment, and explanation of depression changed dramatically throughout human history—it's pretty substantially changed in the last fifty years.[9] It was once the case that *real* depression, as an *illness*, only counted if there weren't certain extenuating life circumstances. Specifically, prior to the changes in the *Diagnostic and Statistical Manual, Fifth Edition*, (*DSM-5*), if you were mourning the loss of a loved one, it didn't count as medical depression, because bereavement is the natural response to difficult circumstances. But in 2013, the "bereavement exclusion" was removed.[10] A form of depression that was once thought to be "normal" now qualifies as an illness.

Maybe you think that it's a bad thing that we have made mourning into a medical condition—a sign that our society can no longer face the basic stresses of life. Or maybe you think it's a good thing that those who once suffered needlessly can receive help.[11] My only point here is that when we expect psychology and psychiatry to work like most other medical fields, we will often be disappointed.

More importantly, in the end, at your point of contact with the world, it always comes down to the same thing. Whether or not you have an official mental illness or disorder, your disorder has been properly diagnosed, or the normal travails of life have overwhelmed you, it always, always, *always* comes to the same thing: the choice to live, which only you can make.

We do a great disservice to one another by overly relying on the technical language of mental health. It ends up demarcating legitimate from illegitimate mental affliction. And if only medically diagnosed mental suffering counts, people will become desperate to find a diagnosis that validates their affliction. But in the end, we're still faced with the same choice: How will you act? All other questions and methods and labels fade into the background when confronted with the question of why we should get out of bed.

Even when you are confident that you have a mental illness, there are no finely articulated lines, no clear objective markers, to tell you where your agency ends and your illness begins– where normal, reasonable sadness ends and your depression begins, for example. Or what is the result of some biochemical problem, and what is the result of a dour personality or self-centered negativity. We have some good theories, but almost nothing is definitive. Good counselors and doctors will tell you this. Pharmaceutical and insurance companies would like us to believe there are objective diagnoses, easy answers, and successful treatments. Sometimes there are, but not usually. We put unrealistic expectations on these fields when we demand objective answers for something so deeply subjective and personal, something that can have genetic, biological, interpersonal, spiritual, economic, and circumstantial causes all at the same time.

If we aren't careful, medical and scientific language can obscure or replace the very thing it's supposed to be treating. It can draw our attention away from the conscious, moment-by-moment responsibility of living by reducing the difficulty of that responsibility to a label. With a diagnosis we try to objectify our suffering, and we hope to place our despair in a nice tidy, medical box. We can set it on a table, examine it, and communicate it to others: I am not depressed. I *have* depression. It is over there and I am over here. My experience has a listing in *DSM-5*. I can name it. So, maybe it's manageable after all?

Except that mental suffering is never "over there." It can't be. By its nature, mental suffering is always experienced subjectively, inside us. And at best, that experience can only be communicated to others in figurative language. "It feels like I'm drowning. Like I'm detached from my body. Like everything is much darker than it used to be." Remarkably, we can even struggle to communicate an episode of mental illness to ourselves once we are past it. The memory remains but not the experience of it. How can something so intensely intimate and vivid become so alien to us? How can your mind be completely consumed by a thought, a fear, an oppressive weight, and yet years or even months later you can remember that period only in glimpses, shadows, the odd mood in the afternoon? But it is never quite the same unless it consumes you again. And then it is all too real.

When you realize all of this, it's not hard to fall into despair. Psychology and psychiatry don't have an answer for why life is worth living despite suffering. They can't shield you from the question by curing you. They can do a great deal to help us manage our mental suffering, whether it counts as a formal, insurance-approved medical diagnosis or not. But we're still left with the same choice. We still have to get out of bed.

Let me be clear: if you are suffering, please get professional help. If you haven't had a good experience with a therapist or a medication, try a new therapist and talk to your doctor about other medications. It takes time to get it right, and it is worth the effort. They may not be able to perfectly explain and cure your illness, but they can provide some meaningful answers and treatments.

Also accept two facts.

First, life is hard. Sometimes it is all-but-unbearably hard. Life can become so painful and monotonous and empty that you cannot begin to comprehend it unless you are right in the middle of it, and even then it doesn't make sense. If you have lived through a season of mental anguish, you almost certainly cannot remember it accurately. There are entire shades of depression and anxiety that are lost to you now. You might be able to recall the day you couldn't go to work because of your depression, or when you had a panic attack in the Target parking lot, but that experience of depression or anxiety remains inaccessible and alien until it returns in force.

And maybe after hearing a sound or catching the light off a windshield on a certain kind of summer day, you'll be suddenly transported back into that mood, some indescribable mixture of self-loathing, dread, sexual vulnerability, and boredom. Or maybe it will be the heat of the sun off asphalt in a decaying strip mall, mixed with the stark defenselessness of childhood, the chemical smell of a certain kind of plastic toy, and a disappointed and tired parent. There are a billion unique ways to blend your senses, experiences, thoughts, and memories. Some shades of depression and anxiety will revisit you, becoming old friends over time. Others will occur once and never again, and you'll only catch haunting glimpses of them when you stumble upon a memory. The human capacity for feeling so many variations of mental suffering is remarkable and sobering.

Human existence inescapably involves suffering. For all of human history we have known this to be true. But it's hard to recall this truth when we are surrounded by forces that promise us greater and greater explanations, control, and strategies of happiness. So, remember this: tremendous suffering is the normal experience of being in this world. Beauty and love and joy are normal, too, but so is suffering.

Second, there are rarely clear answers to depression, anxiety, and other mental health disorders. You can and should pursue professional help, but remember that there are limits. And at those limits we are thrown back on ourselves, God, and our neighbor for the responsibility of living. Even the best counseling and medication cannot replace the existential decision to live and rely on God and your neighbor. Professional help can guide you and medication can assist you—at their best they are means of healing from God—but in the end it is always just you and God and your neighbor and the present choice to act, which at root is actually the choice to worship. And that is okay. Really, it is.

Which brings me back to the point of all this: What does it mean to live? Why should we ever get out of bed?

Lately I have been wondering why
We go to so much trouble to postpone the unavoidable
And prolong the pain of being alive

<small>PEDRO THE LION, "PRIESTS AND PARAMEDICS"</small>

W E QUITE RIGHTLY HEAR regular appeals for people who are struggling with suicidal ideation to get help. And very few serious people advise us to resist the tragedy of human life by ending it early. But there remains the question of what it means to live. Why is it meaningful and good to live? Why put up with all this suffering? Hamlet asks if it is better to endure "the slings and arrows of outrageous fortune" or to end himself.[12] Which is a good question, and one that deserves an answer.

The 2002 Pedro the Lion song "Priests and Paramedics" tells the story of a priest who loses hope and admits in the middle of a funeral, "Lately I have been wondering why we go to so much trouble to postpone the unavoidable and prolong the pain of being alive."[13] Sure, life isn't *only* pain, but it is a lot of pain. And if you don't have an answer to the priest's question when sudden tragedy or prolonged and tedious suffering overwhelm you, it will be too late.

What makes this question difficult to answer is that on balance, there may well be times when your life seems more trouble than it's worth. The pain will outweigh the pleasure. Whatever hopes you have will be overshadowed by your reasonable expectations of suffering. Whatever good you can imagine doing pales before the harm you have already done and will do to others. At times like this, it feels rational to give up on life.

Of course, when you get to this place, you will not be in a rational state of mind. You may think that you are calmly and objectively evaluating whether or not to live or get out of bed, but you won't be. If you speak to friends, they will remind you that you are wrong, that it's the illness talking and life is worth living. But it is difficult to trust the perspective of others when your own impressions are so intense and when it's your existence and suffering that is in question.

This is precisely the situation the nameless wife in Cormac McCarthy's novel *The Road* finds herself in. By every rational materialist calculation, suicide is the most ethical and appropriate response to a world of evil and suffering. She, her husband, and their young son are alive at the end of civilization. The sun is darkened by ash. Nothing grows. Everything and everyone has died or is dying. Every day brings a new horror. There is every reason to believe that even if they manage to fight off starvation and the elements, they will eventually be captured, raped, and eaten alive by cannibals. When she lays out the case for suicide to her husband, he can offer no rebuttal—because there is none.[14] The facts are the facts. Staying alive will lead to greater agony. When you no longer have hope for a pleasurable life, when you have every expectation of increased suffering, suicide is logical—unless the reason we choose to go on living is something greater than pleasure, or freedom from pain, or even hope for a better tomorrow.

And yet her husband refuses to join her, and he prevents her from taking their son with her. Despite the persuasiveness of his wife's argument, despite all the evidence that seems to confirm her decision (the man and his son are very nearly caught by cannibals at least twice after she dies), the father chooses to keep his son alive.

McCarthy forces us, through the father, to grapple with the question at the heart of life: Why is life worth all this agony? And while the father cannot verbally respond to his wife's argument that suicide is the least harmful response to suffering, his embodied answer is powerful and is validated by the ending of the novel.

Why doesn't the man follow his wife? McCarthy gives us at least three reasons, each grounded in a truth beyond the world of the novel. First, the father sees his son as a "warrant" for God's existence, a witness to the goodness of life (and therefore some kind of Life-Giver) even in a world with few other signs of goodness.[15] Second, he believes that God commanded him to protect the life of his son: "My job is to take care of you. I was appointed to do that by God."[16] The father's responsibility to God is not subject to speculations about the possibility of reducing his son's suffering by killing him. Harm reduction is not the ultimate good. What matters to the man, at least by the very end of the novel, is that he fulfills his duty to God to care for the life of his son. Third, the man believes that his own choice to live is a witness to his son that life is good and worth preserving, even through great suffering and the absence of earthly hope: "This is what the good guys do. They keep trying. They dont give up."[17] In fact, I think the testimony of their actions is one of the main reasons the father begs his wife not to kill herself. He knows that once she commits suicide, his son will see that as a real possibility for himself, and he does.

Like the parents in *The Road*, you did not ask to be placed here. As the wife says, "I didnt bring myself to this. I was brought."[18] You did not ask to be a witness to your children and your neighbors. You did not volunteer to be responsible for others or to be your brother's keeper. But none of that really matters. Because here you are, and here they are. And it is good. When the son begins to doubt the goodness of their lives, the father tells him, "I think it's pretty good. It's a pretty good story. It counts for something."[19]

You need to know that your being in the world is a witness, and it "counts for something." Your existence testifies. There is no mitigating this fact. There is nowhere you can hide where your life will not speak something to the world. All we can do sometimes is to decide what our existence is a witness *to*, what it speaks *of*, and how we can share the burden of witnessing with one another.

Many of the truths our lives communicate are beyond our control. For example, because you are made in the image of God, your personhood proclaims the goodness of a Creator God. You can try to denigrate your personhood through self-abuse or self-loathing, but you remain in His image, and so you testify. But there are other areas of our lives that we do have control over. The choices we make in those areas communicate to people. It is those choices I am speaking about here.

When we sin, for example, we not only defy God's law and harm ourselves and wrong our neighbor. We also lie to our neighbor. Our sin proclaims to others that God's promises are not enough.

Consider this in relation to an extramarital affair. If I were to cheat on my wife, what would that act communicate to my children—to my son and daughters? To my students? To my wife? Setting aside for a moment the tremendous harm such a sin would cause to my marriage, and the pain it would cause my family, what would it tell my children about sacred vows? What would it tell them about love and commitment? What would it tell them about desires and contentment? Would not my daughters begin to worry that when they get married, they might not "be enough" for their husbands? Would not my son feel justified in lusting after women when his heart "deeply" desires it? Would not my students and friends begin to imagine infidelity as a bit less scandalous, a bit more normal and reasonable?

Or what if I cursed out a salesperson who refused to give me a refund? What would that communicate about who is worthy of respect?

Or what if I devoted my life to my career, working long hours for years on end, providing a comfortable life for my family, achieving great success in my field, donating to various charities, but giving almost no time to my family, friends, or church? What would that communicate to others about the value of the human person?

All these actions add up. It's not just the lust and infidelity, or the pride and anger, or the greed and vanity. It's the way these sins make sin more plausible for others. When others face similar choices in life, our example will affect their imagination and how they respond.

We almost never take the witness of our actions seriously enough. I suspect that's because if we did, it would frighten us. It's scary to realize that my every decision communicates to people around me something about the nature of God, the goodness of His creation and laws. It means that my sin is never containable. It's never something I can "make right." The effects of my actions ripple throughout time and space, drawing in more and more people, for good and for ill. While God's grace is sufficient for our sins, we do well to recognize the consequences of our sins.

But of all our actions, very few speak louder about the nature of God, His goodness, His love for us, and the goodness of His creation than our choice to get out of bed each morning.

Life will inevitably crush you, at one point or another, and your response to that suffering will testify to something. There will be times when subjectively you will be convinced that life is not worth living, and that existence is not beautiful or good but onerous and meaningless. When those times come, your obligation is to look toward others as witnesses of God's goodness, to remember your responsibilities to care for others, and to remember that you are always a witness, whether you want to be or not. But most of all, remember that you are God's beloved. This means acknowledging the objective reality that life is good, and that despite our distress, we must get up and carry on.

Your existence is a testament, a living argument, an affirmation of creation itself. When you rise each day, that act is a faint but real echo of God's "It is good." By living this life, you participate in God's act of creation, asserting with your very existence that it is a good creation.

The Judge of all has declared His creation—of which you are no small part, no mistake, and no error—to be good. There is no countermanding that declaration. We can choose to accept that our lives are objectively good before God, or we can deny it. We can assent to God's act of creation and preservation, or we can vainly rebel against it. But when we choose to affirm what God has already done in creating us, what God is already doing in granting us breath and in preserving His world and us in it, we worship Him.

Near the end of *The Road*, after the father and son have journeyed south through cold and starvation and encounters with cannibals, the boy asks his father, "What's the bravest thing you ever did?" The father replies, "Getting up this morning."[20]

And he's right. It is brave. It's brave in the world of the novel and in our own world. It's brave to get up knowing that any number of unimagined horrors may greet you. It's brave to get up knowing that your friend or child may suffer those horrors. It's brave to get up when you feel utterly hopeless and yet you obey the demands of your duty to others. It's brave when the father gets up, and it's brave when we do it.

Any action is a step to the block.

T. S. ELIOT, "LITTLE GIDDING"

W E WAGER OUR LIVES through our choices. This is, in part, what I think Paul was getting at when he said that if Christ did not rise from the dead, we are "most to be pitied" (1 Corinthians 15:19). Paul sacrificed his life, his desires, his social status, and his community for the sake of the gospel. He wagered his life. He risked all he had of worldly worth. And if it turned out that Christ was not in fact the Son of God who rose from the dead so that we might have life, then Paul had denied himself for nothing. At the same time, I suspect that many of Paul's Jewish hearers respected his words because they came at a great cost. Any form of evangelism that has nothing at wager has nothing to say.

In *Four Quartets*, T. S. Eliot writes that "any action is a step to the block."[21] He means that our actions always draw us closer to death, and in that sense every action we take is a wager of our time. When I read Eliot's poem, I imagine a wrongly condemned man calmly and decisively walking to the executioner's block with his head held high, maintaining his dignity in the face of injustice. Each step brings him closer to death, but each step is also his own action, taken by his own feet and in defiance of the condemnation he is under. The onlookers observe his defiance and his dignity. His action is a testament that death is not final. That is the difference between a secular stoicism and bravely acting in defiance of our fears and hopelessness. For the stoic, though they can choose to face death bravely, death is the final word. For the Christian, death has been conquered, so we can face it bravely regardless of our fears. We can take a step to the block, confident in our hope.

Likewise, any action we take gambles the limited time we have on earth. We wager all other possible actions by choosing one. Whenever we choose a medical treatment or a school for our kids or a career path, we risk something—being wrong, failure, regret, time, poverty, and so on. Whenever we sin, we wager offense against God and the possibility of uncontainable harm to others (sin is never containable). Whenever, by the power of the Holy Spirit, we turn from sin and choose to honor God and love our neighbor, we wager our fleshly desires. Like Paul, it costs us to obey. To deny sin is to die to self. And that, too, testifies to those watching. It is precisely because our actions are wagers that they communicate something about us and our understanding of the world. They may communicate our trust in the medical community or our trust in public schools or the moral imperative of pursuing our dream jobs. But our actions always speak.

Sometimes the risks of life overwhelm us, and we avoid making a decision. This is especially true in a society like ours, which gives us more and more options. If we can't *know* who to marry or what to do with our lives or which brand of clothing is the most ethically manufactured, maybe we can't do anything at all. Eventually we fold in on ourselves, unable to commit, or only committing to things half-heartedly, exhausted by our own sense of inadequacy. This is despair. We will still move toward the block, but we'll be dragged there against our will.

The most fundamental decision is the decision to get out of bed. And it too communicates something. The decision to get out of bed is the decision to live. It is a claim that life is worth living despite the risk and uncertainty and the inevitability of suffering—one of the few things we can know for certain in this life.

Rising out of bed each day is also a decisive act. Living is a wager. It is a severe gamble. You do not know the suffering and sorrow that awaits. You do not know the heartache. But you know it *is* coming for you: to that, history and literature

41

have testified without counterclaim. To choose to go on is to proclaim with your life, and at the risk of tremendous suffering, that it is good. Even when it is hard, it is good. Even when you don't *feel* that it is good, even when that goodness is unimaginable, it is good.

When we act on that goodness by rising out of bed, when we take that step to the block in radical defiance of suffering and our own anxiety and depression and hopelessness, with our heads held high, we honor God and His creation, and we testify to our family, to our neighbors, and to our friends of His goodness. This act is worship.

This form of worship is one thing I think the apostle Paul has in mind when he exhorts us to "present [our] bodies as a living sacrifice, holy and acceptable to God, which is [our] spiritual worship" (Romans 12:1). We offer our bodies as a living sacrifice by daily embracing life and dying to our flesh: our sinful desires, our selfishness, our pride, even our fear and despair. Unlike the sacrifices offered under the old covenant, which came through death, our sacrifices come through life, from the decision to honor God with our lives. Christ's death is the once-and-for-all sacrifice, and now we participate in that sacrifice by participating in His life. And like properly offered sacrifices in the Old Testament, when we live before Christ, our bodily living sacrifice is a sweet aroma to Him.

The choice to get out of bed is not made once per day but continually as we *do the next thing*. At any moment we may slip back into lethargy, into despair and hopelessness. If we allow ourselves to consider all our obligations, all our responsibilities, all the ways we must perform and improve ourselves, we will become frozen in place. The world asks too much of us. And a good number of these demands really are our responsibility: to care for those around us, to use the gifts God has given us, and so on. In my experience, the only way to move forward is to dedicate yourself to doing the next thing.

To do the next thing is not to deny our other responsibilities but to recognize that faithfulness is always an obligation for the present.[22] Right now we have a duty to serve God by doing *whatever good work He has put before us*. And if we trouble ourselves with all the *other* things we are burdened with, the things of tomorrow or the next hour or minute, we will be overwhelmed. God asks only that we serve Him *now*. Choose this second who you will serve, and then serve Him by doing the next thing. Place it in the forefront of your mind so that you don't lose sight of it: I will get out of bed. Put on my shoes. Walk downstairs. Make coffee. And so on. We have to do all these things without getting lost in perfection, in frantically trying to master our lives by choosing the *perfect* next thing. Very often it is only by focusing on the concrete details of life, the singular actions demanded of us, that we can keep moving.

But when we do the next thing, we communicate with our bodies that the next thing is worth doing. This moment is worth living. This life and all the responsibilities it entails is worth whatever hardships we experience. We need to be reminded of this. So do our neighbors.

Don't confuse doing the next thing *for God*, which is what I'm describing, with living for the sake of living. It is generally true that if you create habits of living, then you will have better mental health. If you get a head of steam, you can get through much of life on pure momentum. If you get up at the same time every day, eat a healthy breakfast, get a sufficient amount of exercise, and go to bed early every night, you will find life more manageable.

Which is fine. But it isn't enough. Living for the sake of living—doing things so that you can continue to efficiently do things—begs the question, Why live? To live. That isn't a sufficient answer. Now or sometime in the future that answer will fall flat for you or someone you love. The mere fact that you *can* cope with great suffering is not in itself a reason to cope with it. So when we encourage depressed and anxious people to be active, get out of the house, and stay busy just so that they'll feel good enough to stay busy, we may help them get out of a funk, but we aren't helping them understand the goodness of their existence. Don't do the next thing just so that you can keep doing the next thing. Do the next thing because it honors God and testifies of His goodness and the goodness of your life to your neighbor.

Moments create momentum. When you choose to do the next thing, neither accepting nor denying the anxiety or depression you carry, you create the momentum that makes the next, next thing a bit easier to manage. And the converse is true. When you cannot do the next thing, everything becomes harder to manage.

When your days are filled with mundane tasks, none of which are worth posting on social media or even talking about, it can feel impossible to build momentum, to feel like your life is *going* anywhere for any purpose. This is precisely why we must see that each choice to do the next thing is an act of worship, and therefore fundamentally good. Feeding your pets is an act of worship. Brushing your teeth is. Doing the dishes. Getting dressed. Going to work. Insofar as each of these actions assumes that this life in this fallen world is good and worth living despite suffering, they are acts of faith in God. Choose to do the next thing before and unto God, take a step toward the block. That is all you must ever do and all you can do. It is your spiritual act of worship.

The practice of getting out of bed, facing the day, and honoring God with your actions is also part of the definition of love given by the apostle Paul in 1 Corinthians. We are most used to hearing these verses read during weddings, as they are a beautiful reminder of the nature of love. Practiced rightly, love turns out to be a great challenge to our egos:

> Love is patient and kind; love does not envy or boast; it is not arrogant or rude. It does not insist on its own way; it is not irritable or resentful; it does not rejoice at wrongdoing, but rejoices with the truth. Love bears all things, believes all things, hopes all things, endures all things. (1 Corinthians 13:4-7)

While these verses are a wonderful reminder of how all married people ought to act toward their spouse, the implications are much broader. They apply to our relationships with friends and even strangers. But here I'd like to suggest something a little different. If this definition of love is accurate, then it also communicates something about the way we ought to interact with God Himself, and therefore how we ought to think about His creation, which includes us. It teaches us how to love ourselves.

If you flinch a little at the idea of loving yourself, I urge you to reconsider. I also cringe a little at this concept. To my ears, it sounds a little too similar to the tautological, vacuous positive thinking and self-esteem talk that I grew up around: you should love yourself because it's important to love yourself. But we should not let the abuse of a concept obscure its truth.

It was only when I read the work of the Christian philosopher Josef Pieper that I became convicted that I really must love myself, that it is an offense to God *not* to love myself. Pieper describes love as the act of saying, "It's *good* that you exist; how wonderful that you are!"[23] And that is true about God's attitude toward us. We know that He delights in our existence because He created us! So how could we not echo His "It is good" by also loving ourselves, by affirming that it is lovely that we exist?

Of course, as we have already thoroughly discussed, this does not mean that we always *feel* pleasure in our lives, or happiness, or delight in our existence. But even when we feel despair, depression, or anxiety, we can *know* that it is good that we exist, and *act* on that knowledge. We love ourselves because we are lovely before God, and what other opinion could possibly matter more than God's? I believe that 1 Corinthians gives us some concrete examples of how we can echo God's delight in our existence by loving ourselves.

Consider what the description of verse seven means for the way we view our lives: "Love bears all things, believes all things, hopes all things, endures all things." To love myself, my neighbor, and God, I must bear all things. Not only all the wrongs and offenses caused by my spouse, family, or even strangers, but also the sufferings I experience internally. The ones brought on by mental illness or the circumstances of life. I bear up under the suffering, resting on God and those closest to me, because in bearing with suffering, I love God by loving myself. And I model for my neighbors how they ought to also love themselves. Similarly, I must believe all things. Maybe most relevantly, I must believe God's love for me is greater and more perfect than my imagination, that He does not make mistakes. That belief is not countermanded by my experience, my emotions, or the opinions of others.

To love myself I must hope all things. This hope is founded on the promises of God, not on my own ability to fix myself or control my circumstances or solve the problems of the world. My hope is in God's promise to preserve me, to work all things together for my good, to finish the good work He started in me. And finally, to love myself properly, I must endure all things—including the torments of my own mind. I may tremble at the agony of life. At times I may feel crushed and overwhelmed and undone, but to love God, I must love myself; and to love my neighbor, I must love myself; and to love myself, I must endure.

I cannot do this alone, however. I bear, believe, hope, and endure not from my own capacity for love but with the aid of the Holy Spirit and with the comfort and encouragement of my friends. It is only with the aid of others that I can love myself and thereby honor God's creation.

≈

So far I have been speaking of this question of whether to get out of bed as a matter of choice. I know that for some people this doesn't seem like a choice at all. When you are sick, you are sick. When you are crushed by the weight of depression, you cannot simply snap out of it. When anxiety constricts your breathing, you can't suddenly choose to be calm. And to treat it as merely a question of *will* brings us right back to where we started: blaming mental illness or suffering on bad character.

And while all that is true, it is also true that the lines between our freedom and the power of a mental illness are murky at best. At the point of contact with the world, when our feet hit the floor, all questions of agency become inconsequential. Freedom and determinism have no bearing or relevance. They belong to a theoretical way of understanding the world, which has its place, but in practice, no person knows where their agency ends. With few exceptions, we experience each moment as if we have a choice of how we will act. Even when our minds suffocate us with hopelessness and we feel unable to move, we still experience the ability to choose. Whether or not that freedom is real, or to what extent we can choose in the midst of a panic attack or great despair are fascinating theoretical questions. But so long as we experience the ability to choose, we have the responsibility to act on that ability. Because more basic and essential, more true and real than any psychological explanation of suffering or illness, is our raw, day-to-day experience of living.

Acknowledging our responsibility to get out of bed and live does not mean that we can condemn those who reject that responsibility. When someone loses their life to a mental illness, it is not our place to question whether they fought hard enough, whether it was *really* the illness or a weakness in their character. The truth is that many faithful, strong, godly people have been so broken by their trauma or mental illness that they have succumbed to suicide. And Christ's work on the cross is more than sufficient for them, just as it is sufficient for your grievous sins and mine. It is presumptuous and uncharitable for us to judge their actions. God is Judge, not us. The experience of mental suffering is always incommunicable —except to God. So no matter how well you think you know someone and their illness, remember that you know very little—far too little to judge them.

Instead, we ought to focus on two things that *are* our business. First, we ought to bear one another's burdens. We can't save someone else, but we are responsible to love our neighbor. You may need to sit with someone through a particularly dark night to ensure that they don't harm themself. You may need to help them check in to an inpatient program.

You may need to ask them difficult questions about suicidal thoughts and plans, or ensure that they don't have access to a gun. You certainly need to pray with and for them.

Second, we must not excuse or overlook our sin because of a mental affliction. Your affliction does not give you the right to hurt other people, to abuse them, to neglect them, or to mistreat yourself. You have no business judging the sincerity of someone else's fight against depression and suicide, but you do have a responsibility to endure suffering without excusing sin in your own life.

Life is an awesome responsibility and burden. The uncomfortable truth is that suicide becomes a slightly more viable option for people when someone they respect succumbs to it. If you give up, it will open up the possibility for others to give up, whether "giving up" means suicide or apathy. You have the solemn responsibility and privilege to bear witness to the goodness of life by living despite suffering. Like the father in *The Road* whose every action is judged by his watching son, there are vulnerable, frightened people watching you, waiting to see how you will endure.

And don't think you can control who witnesses your life, like a celebrity carefully curating their public image—as if you could contain your life, hiding the shameful parts so that they only affect you. That's not how life works. You are not your own, and neither is your suffering. In this world you will encounter untold numbers of people in circumstances beyond your knowledge and control. It's entirely possible that the ones watching you most closely are total strangers.

You didn't ask for this. I didn't either. But who said we get to volunteer to be our brother's keeper? Where did we get the idea that our responsibilities to one another are optional, rather than given by God? The man in *The Road* believes God appointed him to care for his son, and so we are appointed to care for our neighbors. This is a hard teaching, but we are responsible for one another, even when we are in the midst of great suffering and sorrow.

But life is also a gift. And as it turns out, the greatest gifts are always also burdens: love, wisdom, beauty, salvation, children. Our being is a result of gratuitous love by God, and we honor that gift by participating fully in it, even when participating in being feels unbearable.

None of this is to imply that suicidal ideation and depression are trivial matters that we can just pray away or "snap out" of. But it does mean that for Christians who understand that the preservation of our life is an essential act of God's love for us, suicide is not an option we can entertain. We can admit that we and many others have struggled and will continue to struggle with it—some thorns in the flesh won't come out this side of paradise. But part of facing despair is knowing how we ought to respond. And since our life is a gift of grace and a witness to the goodness of life, and therefore the goodness of the Creator, ending our life must never be a possibility, no matter how strongly we subjectively feel dread, alienation, or fear. We have an obligation to live in the truth, not that our actions redeem us or our neighbor. We act out of gratitude for the sacrifice Christ made for us. And this gratitude will sometimes be felt in your bones and sometimes not be felt at all. But you can still choose to act on that gratitude, embracing the gracious gift of life.

Our hope is not in an immediate "cure" or release from all mental affliction but that in the fullness of time, we will be made whole. In 1 Peter 5:7, Peter writes a command that is often used as an easy solution to anxiety. He calls us to cast "all your anxieties on him, because he cares for you." In the larger context of his letter, Peter is talking to persecuted Christians. Their "anxieties" weren't rooted in mental disorders but ongoing religious persecution. While I think this verse can be misused to dismiss anxiety as a trivial problem ("Maybe you should just cast your anxieties on Him!"), I do think the wider passage speaks to the common human experience of suffering.

Peter begins with a series of commands:

> Humble yourselves, therefore, under the mighty hand
> of God so that at the proper time he may exalt you,

casting all your anxieties on him, because he cares for you. Be sober-minded; be watchful. Your adversary the devil prowls around like a roaring lion, seeking someone to devour. Resist him, firm in your faith, knowing that the same kinds of suffering are being experienced by your brotherhood throughout the world. (1 Peter 5:6-9)

When we are experiencing anxiety, commands are rarely what we want to hear. We feel overwhelmed enough as it is. But I think these commands can help reorient us so that we can endure.

Take the command to humble yourself. If you are suffering with a mental illness or distressing life circumstance, you might already feel incredibly weak and small, incapable of moving or making decisions—which sounds a lot like humility. But I think Peter has something else in mind. To accept that your life is a good gift from a loving God, you must trust God. You must accept that your existence is a blessing even when it seems like a curse. Sometimes the humility you need is not a kind of smallness of spirit or sense of your own weakness but the faith to act as if your life is a blessing—because it is. Similarly, I take the command to cast our anxieties on God not as a simplistic solution to hand over our psychological experience of anxiety, but as *acting* on the belief that it is God who cares for us, that in fact we can't care for ourselves. That is the lesson at the center of Christianity: we cannot live a fully human life apart from God. The practice of offering our anxieties to God may not make them disappear, but it will remind us that we are in the hands of our loving Father.

The next commands, to be sober-minded, to be watchful, and to resist the devil, are good reminders that living with mental affliction requires vigilance. The devil would like nothing more than to persuade you that your life is meaningless, for it is in the destruction of what God has made good that the devil seeks to defy God. Practically, resisting may look like talking to yourself: making a habit of identifying and denying thoughts of worthlessness, hopelessness, and despair. The goal is not to reason your brain out of despair. That rarely works, in my experience. Instead, it's to form habits that in their very nature affirm what you know to be true when you don't feel it to be true. When you are tired, sick, stressed, burned out from doing some thankless good work— any time you are vulnerable to self-doubt—be ready to label it as the lie it is and move on. You'll probably still feel bad, but that's okay. Just do the next thing in faith.

The command that provides me the most comfort is the last one: remembering that your suffering is unique but not special. I suppose that's sort of the point of this little book. Whatever you are going through, an element of that pain is inexpressible. Your personal experience of illness, or mental suffering, or trauma is unique. It happened to you in ways that only you and God can understand. But that doesn't mean it's special. If you come to believe that your suffering is yours alone, you will believe that *you* are the problem. The world would be better off without you because you are the one who is messed up, who can't seem to get it together.

But no, Peter says. Whatever you are going through, the world is filled with people suffering similarly. There are unique qualities to your experience, but you aren't alone. There are *Christians* suffering in similar ways all over the world. Some suffer much less than you, some suffer more than you can imagine, but this burden of life is something we carry in common. So when you feel worthless or overwhelmed with anxiety, it's not a sign that you lack faith or are not a true or good Christian. Millions of your brothers and sisters in Christ feel the same way right now. But there is another implication: if our suffering is common, then we should not hide it but instead help others bear it.

After all these commands, Peter offers a beautiful promise: "And after you have suffered a little while, the God of all grace, who has called you to his eternal glory in Christ, will himself restore, confirm, strengthen, and establish you. To him be the dominion forever and ever. Amen" (1 Peter 5:10-11). These verses can be misused to shame people who continue to have a mental thorn in the flesh: "If you just humbled yourself and cast your cares properly, then your suffering would only last 'a little while'!" But Peter is absolutely correct. Whatever you are suffering, it *will* only last a little while. That little while may be a week, or it may be your entire life. How is that comforting? Because the ending is already written: you will overcome, Christ has redeemed and will glorify you, including your flawed and, in some cases, ill mind.

When you are in a period of deep despair, one of the doubts that plagues you is the fear that you will never get out. You are too broken, too wicked, too weak—you have wasted too much time and squandered too many of God's gifts to redeem your life. But Peter reminds us that this is one of the most fundamental lies of the devil—that we are without hope. The "little while" you suffer in this life may very well last a lifetime. Suffering is a normal part of life. But you can remind yourself that it is not the ultimate truth. It ends. And it ends not with your failure or destruction but with a resurrection. And there, if not before, God *will* "restore, confirm, strengthen, and establish you." Until then, we get out of bed, and we do the next thing.

This is not stoicism but an acknowledgment that an essential part of life is bearing with suffering with the knowledge that suffering does not have the final say. And even when our minds deceive us into hopelessness, we cannot shake the truth that life is still precious. Perhaps we cannot sense the preciousness of our own lives, but the lives of our loved ones feel inherently sacred. We love them, which means we feel the goodness of their existence even when we can't feel the goodness of our own. And in those moments we must remember that the decision to scorn the goodness of our own life is always an invitation for others to scorn their lives too. As much as you may wish to isolate your despair to yourself; as much as you may wish to make your worthlessness or misery a special, private case; as much as you may feel your meaninglessness applies only to you—that is not how we are perceived.

Unfortunately, tragic circumstances, your fallen mind, and the devil will all whisper to you that your life is not a gift, that it is not an act of divine love from a God who knows you perfectly and loves you still. And while you can't force yourself to stop *feeling* hopeless, you can sometimes (more often than we'd like to admit) choose to act on the truth of hope.

And the thing is, as J. D. Salinger's Zooey says, "There are really nice things in this world. I mean nice things. We're all such morons to get sidetracked. Always focused on our ego."[24] You can get lost in your own head (trust me) and in your ego. When that happens, if you try to think your way out of being egotistical, you'll only dig yourself in deeper. You must take a step to the block. You must do the next thing. And when you do, eventually you will remember that there are really nice things in this world. And you'll feel like a moron for getting sidetracked in your own head. But that's okay. There's grace for us morons.

You must try to see the nice things around you now. You cannot wait until life slows down, or you feel better, or you are cured or free or whatever to accept the good gifts God gives you. You can't. This is nonnegotiable. In my experience, with few exceptions, life doesn't slow down, and some things don't "get better." You either choose to receive the beauty and wonder of this life in the midst of chaos and distress or you never will.[25]

As soon as you decide in your heart to spurn God's gifts—beauty, love, a good meal, laughter, and so on—because you feel unworthy or unfit, you are denying the reality of God's grace. For what else is the pleasure of good food and laughter with friends and a walk on a beautiful path but the means of grace through which God nurtures us? God is feeding our souls by giving us tastes of hope that defy the oppression of our spirits. Do not mock God's grace by rejecting it for your own suffering.[26]

But the real grace is that these gifts—chief among them the Lord's Supper—are means of grace whether we recognize them or not. Laughter's mighty rebuke to sorrow and despair is not silent even when we ourselves are silent and unable or unwilling to laugh. You don't have to do anything except stretch out your hand and open your eyes and receive.

I know even that can be difficult. Why can't we just get out of our heads for even one minute and delight in the nice things of this life without feeling guilty or unworthy or critical? It's ridiculous, but I think most people would rather try to take pleasure in something pitiful and degrading and self-destructive than sit still and accept grace. Sometimes the best we can do is make the choice to act as if this life is a gift. That honors God. And if we make a practice of it, a practice of defying our anxiety and depression by getting out of bed and just giving a few moments of silent prayer of thanks for this life that maybe we still loathe—that pleases God. It gives hope to people you don't even know. In time you'll start to feel it, too, and if you don't, at least you did what was right.

So—why get out of bed? Why "postpone the unavoidable and prolong the pain of being alive"?[27] Because life itself is a good gift given by a loving God who even now preserves your every breath. Because your life and the lives of those around you are living testaments to God's love, and to destroy that testament would be to make a mockery of God and to lie to your neighbor about the sacredness of their life. And you have a responsibility to use this life to care for your neighbor. And because there are "really nice things in this world," if we can just get out of the way and see them.

Is Richard now himself again?

Robert Lowell, "Home After Three Months Away"

To LIVE THROUGH MENTAL SUFFERING, you must have an answer for why life is worth all the anguish. But if your suffering is from a chronic mental illness (diagnosed or not), then answering this question once isn't enough. You also need to know *how to live* with the mundane burden of a mental illness. Because answering this question doesn't make your depression or anxieties or fears disappear.

Tomorrow you will have to get out of bed again. And the next day. And the day after that. You have to go grocery shopping. And go to work. Read to your children. Help your friend move. Do your homework. Finish that project. Pray and read the Bible. Exercise. Go outside. Eat. In other words, we don't answer this question once in some dramatic moment of revelation that clarifies our lives forever. The choice to live is made every moment of every day, consciously or unconsciously. And in the midst of chronic suffering, whether in the form of a mental illness or a lingering life tragedy that weighs on your spirit, making the conscious choice to get out of bed grows stale and wearisome.

Occasional panic attacks, breakdowns, and depressive episodes can be terrifying, but the monotonous grind of chronic mental suffering is its own kind of burden. You grow used to your illness. It becomes a familiar friend, so that when you have periods of relief you don't *feel* relief—you feel out of sorts, disoriented, or guilty, like you're missing something. A momentary experience of joy or innocent pleasure can make you feel worse, as your disordered mind frantically searches for a reason why you should feel bad, or why you don't deserve this nice thing. Or you are afraid to hope because at any moment the darkness may return, and then you start hoping for the darkness so that you won't be disappointed. So here's the challenge: how to live daily, moment by moment, with a thorn in your flesh.

∾

To live with a chronic mental illness is to always be on edge. Some days your illness will fade into the background and you'll feel "normal" for a minute, but then you'll remember how bad things can get. You'll hear something or see something and the specter of your disease will reappear and you'll realize that you might relapse, that tomorrow you may be stuck in bed or otherwise incapacitated. There's the added anxiety of watching it unfold, feeling the beginnings of a familiar descent, anticipating the decline, rehearsing the same reassurances from your loved ones, wondering how long it will last. And behind all this anxiety is the fear that maybe this time you won't make it out, that you'll finally get lost in your own mind.

Living with a mental illness looks a lot like falling into the same hole day after day. It's mundane and awful and tedious and inexplicable to those around you. It gets old fast. "Is Richard now himself again?"[28]

When you first receive a diagnosis, you can feel a sense of novelty: the assurance that you really *aren't* supposed to feel this way, and it's tragic that you do, and you'll just need to follow the treatment plan and things will get better. While we have good treatments for most mental disorders, there aren't many *cures*, so the monotony gets old pretty quick. The patience your loved ones had for you begins to wear down.

The first time you have an episode, your loved ones don't know what to do. There is alarm and fear, an urgency to get you help, prayers and concern. But then it comes back again. And again. And again. Or maybe it never really left. It always feels intense and real to you because the *experience* is real even if your fears and anxieties are irrational. But to your loved ones it's just more senseless drama. No matter how understanding they are, the daily experience of putting up with your illness is tedious (at best). Although they know it's the illness talking, or the disorder affecting you, they also know that to some extent you still have agency. That blurry line between where your choices end and the disorder takes over is the elephant in the room. No matter how hard you try to get control of your mind, you can never be certain that you did enough. And when you tell them that you are doing your best to fight it, they can never be certain that you're telling the truth, because you aren't certain either. So your patience for yourself wears down too. You are stuck living.

Especially for those who suffer from depression or anxiety, when your suffering gets bad enough, it can feel like the world should stop or people should stop being happy—like everyone should be as depressed or anxious or guilt-ridden as you feel. The vivid intensity of your condition entirely remakes reality so that anyone who doesn't share your suffering seems profoundly incongruous with your world. You may be on antidepressants, but when you are depressed and everyone around you doesn't share your dread, it kind of feels like they are the drugged ones. But no one cares. Nothing happens. You just feel bad and nothing changes.

T. S. Eliot, who knew quite a bit about living with mental suffering, wrote, "People change, and smile: but the agony abides."[29] The agony is bad, but the abiding is what gets to you.

Part of the nightmarish quality of mental illness comes from the fundamental disconnection between the way you experience the world and the way everyone else seems to experience it. You'll be going through the worst episode of your life and discover that nothing changes for anyone else. They don't feel bad. They enjoy books, food, or sex. They pray easily. They find comedies funny. And you'll want to yell at them, "Look around. Do you not see how profoundly terrible and empty this all is? How guilty and inadequate we are? Why aren't you worried? Why aren't you panicked? What's the point of doing anything?" You may find yourself pitying them in their ignorance, but more often you'll find yourself irritated. Their joy makes your own despondency seem all the more dramatic by contrast, which is why it's often hard to be around happy people when you feel bad. The sound of your own children giggling and being silly can feel like nails on a chalkboard.

But as disconnected and irritated as you feel, the truth remains that some of these people still depend on you. A lot of them do. They are still your family, your neighbors, your responsibilities. You don't cease to be part of a community just because your mind is betraying you. The life that goes on around you still involves and requires your attention. The agony abides and so do your responsibilities.

You can be having a breakdown in the bathroom and your kid will knock on the door to ask for a glass of water. Or the dog will need to go outside. Or your roommate will have a bad day at work, and all they need is for you to listen sympathetically while they verbally process it all. Or a lonely friend will call. None of these are unfair or unreasonable requests. They are natural and even good parts of belonging to a community and being human. You can't expect or ask your community to absolve you of your responsibility to them, of your *love* for them, just because you are in mental agony.

There may be times when you have to ask for grace, for a temporary suspension of your normal responsibilities so that you can collect yourself and get some measure of healing. This is healthy and a way to love others by caring for yourself. But if you wait until you are "in a good place" mentally before you accept your responsibilities, you may never act. It's never a good time to sacrifice for others, but it's always the right time to sacrifice for others.

To live with a mental illness is to live in two different realities: the reality of your mental state and the reality of your embodiment in a community. You can no more deny your community than you can deny your mental illness.

Your responsibilities to others cannot make your suffering disappear any more than your mental state excuses you from your responsibilities. The challenge is to live in this tension, to honestly and accurately discern when you need to step away from certain responsibilities in order to heal, and when you need to bear those responsibilities with your suffering for the sake of others. There are no easy answers, and unfortunately, your mind will deceive you. It may insist that you press on when you need to rest and seek professional intervention. And it may use your illness as an excuse to hurt those around you, to treat them as objects or problems standing in your way.

We do know a few things, however. We know that we belong to a community and have a responsibility to them. We know that God loves us and desires us to love others. And we know that failing to care for ourselves (mentally or physically) is also a failure to love others. In times of doubt, when you are unsure if you are being too hard or too easy on yourself, pray for wisdom and discernment. And then act. Whatever state you are in, however you might be suffering, there is a way for you to love others right now. There are responsibilities you *can* handle. However small they might be, take them up.

I hope you never experience this, but you can get to a place where virtually all responsibilities are overwhelming—when you can neither work nor care for yourself. In such times of crisis, when you are suicidal or so crippled by your mental illness that you cannot act, you will need to lay down nearly all of your obligations in order to get the help you need. But even then, laying down your day-to-day obligations is actually a greater way to love God and your neighbor, because it allows you the rest you need to carry on. So never, *ever* feel guilty for seeking help. If your existence is a good creation of a loving God, then you honor God by caring for that creation.

For most people, however, mental illness does not come in periods of absolute crisis requiring hospitalization or intervention. It comes in constant or near-constant, fluctuating, redundant, tedious suffering. And aside from some brief periods of grace to recuperate, you will need to keep actively caring for those around you even when you want to hide and give up on everything.

∿

Mental illness gives you no easy answers. On the one hand, you cannot shame yourself and carry around guilt for being a burden to others. Your burden is a blessing for them to bear (they might not always agree, but it's true anyway). It is pride and selfishness not to allow others to enter into your suffering. Who are you to hinder someone's chance to sacrificially love you? Besides, none of us can make it without the help of others.

But you have the responsibility to care for others as well, which means you need to bear—or at least endure—your own burden as well as you can. A refusal to rely on others is prideful and unloving. It is a failure to "believe all things"—to believe what God has already pronounced over you, that you are His beloved child. A refusal to endure and care for those around you as best you can is prideful and unloving. It is a failure to "bear all things" and "endure all things"—to accept the work of the Holy Spirit in your life, giving you the strength to persevere and serve others.

I know those last sentences will be troubling to a lot of people. I wish it were simpler and we could objectively know *how much* we can do and *how much* we need others.

When I was in my early thirties, I had two herniated discs in my neck surgically fused together to save my spinal cord from being severed. I spent the next three months in a neck brace. I was in graduate school and was teaching two courses. My wife was also teaching two courses, and we had two small children. According to the doctor's instructions, I could not lift anything over ten pounds. For three months I could not carry my infant son. We lived twenty-four hours from family, and while we had a wonderful church community to help us, my wife had to bear most of the burden of caring for our children by herself. I was helpless.

But the nice thing was that we *knew* I was helpless. And my wife knew that if I picked up one of our crying children, I could do serious damage to my spine. So, while I felt bad that I was unable to help, there was a lot of comfort in knowing my limits. I knew that by following the doctor's instructions, I was serving my family. By allowing my body to heal, I was fulfilling my responsibilities as a father.

With mental illness, there is no neck brace to visually communicate the burden you're carrying. And there are almost no objective limits. There's no way for a psychologist to objectively measure your agency or your capacity to work. They can make recommendations, even wise recommendations, but they fundamentally can't separate your abilities from your illness. That means you have to live in the space of uncertainty between the knowledge that your illness limits your agency and the knowledge that you still have agency—between the responsibility to rely on others and the responsibility to care for others. Any way you try to avoid this tension will end in more harm. If you refuse to have grace for yourself or to accept help from others, you will fall deeper into despair and have less and less strength to care for those around you. If you refuse to accept and act on your responsibility to care for the people around you, you will lose yourself in your own helplessness.

~

Here's the kind of thing that can happen to you.

One night in December a father I know was watching his young children while his wife was away. Anxiety seized him so tightly that he could not think about anything else. He could not hear his children's questions. He could not recognize the words in the bedtime story he was supposed to be reading. He could not remember the rest of their bedtime routine. All he could do was try to breathe.

So he told his children, "Daddy's not feeling well. Please be quiet for a few minutes." Then he hid in the bathroom, anxiously running over the same thoughts again and again.

Without supervision, the children ran wild, yelling and arguing and wrestling so that the father finally had to drag himself out of the bathroom. He told them that he was feeling *very* bad, and that he needed them to be responsible and get ready for bed. Still unable to stop his anxiety, he went up to his room and lay face down on the bed. With every passing minute he felt more and more like a failed father and yet helpless to do or be otherwise. All he wanted was to get up, but all he felt was stuck.

And then, from downstairs he began to hear his children's voices. They were singing Christmas carols. Then he heard

71

the sounds of dishes being washed by hand and a vacuum cleaner running over rugs. And Christmas carols.

After nearly an hour of staring into his pillow, the door to his bedroom slowly opened and a child quietly peeked in and asked the father if he could text their mother so they could have a grownup around. However unfit this father had felt before, he felt worse now, as if he had abdicated his role as father and his children knew it and now they were scared to be alone. Only this feeling and his child's frightened face were enough to overcome the anxiety and bring him downstairs, where he told the children that Daddy was okay, but sometimes Daddy's mind didn't work right, but that he'd always be here and always love them.

The father still felt like a failure, and the anxiety still pounded in his head, screaming for attention. But he held his children and read to them and put them to bed.

Your loved ones don't stop needing you just because you're suffering and stuck in your head or pinned to the bed. You can't know exactly how much freedom you have to fight back against the darkness, against your own mind, and choose to be present with those who need you. But you must try. Because you love them, you cannot ask them to suffer needlessly for you. You can't leave them alone while you lose yourself in despair.

You don't get to renounce your brother and sister, or your son and daughter, or your friends and neighbors, even when you feel like you have nothing to give them. To the best of your ability—which is more than you imagine and less than the moment demands—you must set aside your suffering to bear the burdens of others, because the world cannot and will not stop for you. And it *needs* you, whether or not you want it to need you.

It may be that you feel less and less adequate to the task of loving and serving others. It may be that you feel so broken by a mental disorder that you are unfit to be a parent or a spouse or a brother or sister or a neighbor of any kind. But that is a lie. No, you can't bear the weight of the world on your shoulders, but neither can you deny the efficacy of your paltry offering of love.

Choosing to remain present with your friends, to take the dog out, to listen patiently to your coworker even while your mind is screaming and you want to hide or pound your head until it stops—such things are small offerings, small sacrifices, little acts of defiance against your suffering, that may mean the world to them. And anyway, those small offerings are all that God asks of you.

In such moments, the friend or the dog or the coworker may never know what you are sacrificing to be with them. They may not appreciate what you can give them. They may even be confused or frustrated that you cannot do more, but that doesn't matter. What matters is that before God you acted faithfully in doing the next thing. You took a step to the block. You rose out of bed. Such are the unaccountable moments of courage which mental illness—and life itself—demands of us.

∼

Let me tell you what this might look like.

You're standing in the middle of the YMCA swimming pool, holding your daughter's hand because she doesn't know how to swim, and your other kids are swimming laps and going down the slide and enjoying themselves. Besides holding your daughter's hand, all you can do is silently pray the Lord's Prayer so that your mind doesn't collapse back into despair. If you were in a better place mentally, you'd smile and laugh. You'd cheer your kids on and actively help your daughter learn to swim. But today, what you can do is be physically present and devote yourself to not descending.

And the thing is, that's enough. Maybe the entire outing is agonizing to you, and you keep checking the clock on the wall, waiting until you can take them home. But for now, you are *here*. To do the next thing hurts, and you know that you are still not nearly the parent you ought to be, but you are doing the next thing. Holding her hand. Pulling her through the water. Occasionally you smile at her while you continue to soundlessly recite the Lord's Prayer. And in the end, it's nice for them.

Maybe it seems petty to you that anyone would take it as a victory to drag themselves to a swimming pool with their kids, but that's what a mental disorder can do to you. That's what *life* can do to you. Maybe instead of taking your kids to the pool, you'll make the decision to listen to your friend who is going through a terrible breakup, even though you desperately want to crawl into a hole. Or maybe you'll help a frustrated customer at your job, treating them like a human rather than a problem to be resolved, even though your mind is pounding and your gut aches with anxiety.

Whoever you are, wherever you are, there is an opportunity to lovingly and sacrificially attend to someone else. Your mental illness will demand all of your attention. But you don't always have to give it. You can try to make space for others. And you need to try because other people really need you. They might not know it or say it. Your kids may not thank you for taking them to the pool. But they need you. And what it says to them is that this life is worth living, even when it hurts. Your friend's broken heart deserves to be comforted, even when your own heart races with anxiety. That customer's humanity makes them worthy of dignity and kindness, even when you don't feel you have anything left to give. Your life is a witness.

∽

None of this means that you ought to keep your burdens to yourself, whether they are in the form of a mental illness or some other form of mental affliction. During a particularly difficult time in my life, I had to call a couple friends daily just to hold it together. Without warning I called one of these men five minutes before I had to teach class because I was frozen with anxiety and couldn't teach or do anything else. Thanks to his comfort, I taught the class. I think it was even a good class. After weeks of these daily calls, I felt extraordinarily guilty for taking up their time, and I began to apologize repeatedly. But they told me to stop. One said to me, "Alan, I signed up for this years ago when I became your friend. Don't ever apologize for needing help." Those words cut me every time I remember them. And of course he was right. I didn't want to accept it at the time, but he was right.

Enduring requires you to share your suffering with others. If you have children, they need to know something of your struggle. They will notice something is wrong anyway. And they need to see you endure. Talk to your pastor or loved ones or friends. Hiding your suffering from everyone is no better (and can be a good deal worse) than prioritizing your suffering above theirs. They won't have that chance if you lie to them or pretend that everything's great when it's not. Enduring doesn't mean fake smiles and denial of suffering.

It also doesn't mean dramatizing your condition or leveraging it for attention. Maybe it sounds insensitive or offensive to suggest that some people fall in love with their own mental suffering. I suppose it is offensive—but it is also a real temptation. Not for everyone, but I suspect that a significant portion of the people with a mental affliction in America also take some kind of pleasure from it, occasionally at least. This is counterintuitive because anyone who experiences mental anguish will quickly tell you that they desperately want it to end. And they aren't lying. But the human heart is far more complex and contradictory than we admit. It is possible to loathe and be deeply ashamed of our mental state while at times feeling a kind of validation from it, a sense that our experience is somehow more significant or dramatic than "normal life" because of our burden, especially if we have a diagnosis. Or perhaps it relieves us of the unbearable pressure of our highly competitive meritocracy to know that we are not "normal."

As he reflected on the death of his son, Ralph Waldo Emerson observed that "there are moods in which we court suffering."[30] It's a remarkable thing to say given the

77

circumstances. You would never go to a father who has just lost his young son and say to him, "I think you are courting suffering." And yet this is precisely what Emerson said about himself. Both things can be true. You can suffer for legitimate reasons (a personal tragedy, an ailment, a mental illness), and you can go *beyond* that suffering or come to desire it because in some petty, perverse way you find the illness comforting. And whenever we suffer, we long to be comforted.

Emerson speculated that when we pursue suffering, we hope to "find reality, [the] sharp peaks and edges of truth."[31] You may discover, through therapy or deep introspection, that the very anxiety you dread is a kind of familiar friend, something awful but predictable. Something overwhelming but containable. Something, in other words, a little less frightening than the things you fear to fear: inadequacy, being alone forever, failing your loved ones, being a fraud, being unloved by God.

If all of this sounds unfamiliar, good for you. It is not pleasant to discover that you have come to love the condition by which you are tormented. It is even less pleasant to discover that you sometimes find satisfaction in the drama of suffering. But both are very unsurprising human experiences. Our hearts are capable of incredible contortions, especially when we are desperate for affirmation or to feel alive. And it is not uncommon for us to desire the things that hurt us most.

Your suffering does not make you special. It does not make your life more interesting, significant, compelling, or heroic. It doesn't make for a better story. It doesn't even make you worthy of love or compassion. What makes you worthy of love and compassion is the objective reality that God created you in His image and is preserving you *right now*. Neither a wildly successful life of fame and achievements nor a painfully tragic life of suffering and misfortune makes you any more valued, any more alive, or any more worthy of life. We too often turn to self-destructive habits in a desperate effort to *feel* like we have the very thing we always already have: a life that means something real.

But as dangerous as "courting suffering" can be, we can't use it as an excuse to keep our suffering to ourselves. A false humility says that you shouldn't share your burdens, because if you do you may feed your ego or come to find the attention addictive. This isn't an easy tension to hold. It's easier to keep your problems to yourself or to turn them into social capital or a source of perverse comfort. The hardest but most loving thing is to speak honestly and personally, sharing your burdens with those who have earned your trust—neither advertising nor hiding your burdens. Neither looking to your suffering for significance nor denying your need for help. And never apologize for needing help.

The way you carry yourself during periods of mental affliction will communicate to people around you where your hope lies. And the sad truth is that whatever darkness you may be in right now will also be experienced (in one form or another) by your friends, your children, the other members of your small group Bible study, your classmates—anyone and everyone around you. While it is terrible (and occasionally horrifying) to be under a cloud of depression or anxiety, you also have the chance to testify to God's goodness. By watching you endure, others will know that it is possible to keep going. They will have a model for perseverance. You don't know whose life you may save by honestly and faithfully enduring a mental affliction.

Breathe, keep breathing

Don't lose your nerve

RADIOHEAD, "EXIT MUSIC (FOR A FILM)"

I UNDERSTAND THAT WHAT I AM SPEAKING ABOUT is painful and difficult. It would be easier to ignore the unavoidable tensions of mental suffering. When your mind turns against you, the last thing you want to hear is that you need to fulfill a responsibility. Yet this is our calling: to glorify God by honoring His creation—*you*.

You *are* God's good creation—regardless of how you feel or what you have done or experienced or thought. Weakened by sin, fallen, and in need of a Redeemer, yes, but nevertheless your existence in this world is *good*. And even that weakness, that sin, that temptation to spurn God's gift of life, the knowledge that you are selfish and greedy and lustful and always, always so ungrateful—all of that has been overcome by Christ's sacrifice on the cross. The very same God who created you in an act of grace and who preserves you in an act of grace suffered so that you can be redeemed by an act of grace. He desires that none should perish (2 Peter 3:9). That's a remarkable word.

But this isn't primarily about you. As you choose each day to act faithfully in the gift of life God has given you, you affirm the goodness of all His creation. You testify through your actions that your neighbor's life is good, that your child's life is a beautiful gift, and that your friends' lives are instances of God's grace. For if *you* are not God's good creation, then neither am I and neither is anyone else. And if that's the case, I really don't know what we are doing putting up with all this suffering.

Your life is a witness to the value of your neighbor's life. The converse is also true: your neighbor's life is a witness to the beauty of your life. And this can help ground us when we get lost in our hopelessness. While we might wish that everyone around us reflected our hopelessness when we are depressed or our dread when we are anxious, it is generally much easier for us to recognize the value of someone else's life. But we must go a step further and recognize that their lives are valuable and good not because they are better than you, or more worthy, or because they suffer less. Your friend's life is good because it was created by God. Whenever your mind turns against you and you begin to doubt the value of your life, remember those around you. Your life is precious for the very same reason their lives are.

The father in *The Road* regularly wonders whether his own life is worth living, but his firm conviction that his *son's* life is a gift helps him persevere. In that way, his son is a witness to God's love simply by existing. The same is true for us.

But unfortunately, there may come a time when all life feels meaningless—when you cannot believe that existence is a sacred gift from God, when you can no longer even believe in the objective goodness of other people's lives. I hope that you never experience this. It is a kind of hell. There are three things I want you to understand if you ever find yourself in this place.

First, for any number of reasons (biological, cultural, economic, experiential), your mind is in denial about the fundamental nature of reality. The miracle of creation is evident everywhere, including in your existence, but in despair your mind sees only meaningless suffering. In such times, you can't force yourself to snap out of it, but you can remind yourself that your mind is lying to you.

Second, if you find yourself in total despair, you must surrender to the grace of your neighbors, particularly wise and loving friends within the local church. You must learn to accept their love for you and their words of assurance, which may not heal you but can carry you when you are incapable of carrying yourself. Sometimes your duty in life is simply to trust and rely on the love of others. Most of the time, really.

Third, I'm so sorry. It will be okay. Hold on.

Sometimes the right use of your agency is to surrender part of it to others for a period. That may look like prolonged inpatient treatment. It may look like calling a friend who reminds you that your life and their life and every life created by God is a work of grace, and that your task is to just do the next thing you need to do today and endure the burden of despair until it dissipates, or at least slackens. It may look like trusting your doctor and family members who assure you that your prescribed medications are both necessary and good for you.

It may also look like accepting that you need medical help. This can be frightening and humbling. Far too many of us try to carry our suffering alone, unwilling to seek "professional help" because of the stigma surrounding mental disorders, or fears of what we might discover through therapy, or fears that medication will change our personality. We may also fear that going to therapy or seeing a psychiatrist will prove that we are broken in some way. No one wants to be broken. So we think to ourselves, *If I can just hold out a bit longer, maybe this episode of mental suffering will pass, and I won't have to bother with therapy*. Because we think if we must get *professional* help, then this suffering is a real problem. It's not just a season. Even more frightening, what if we get treated and nothing gets better? Then we are truly hopeless.

While it's true that receiving a diagnosis is not a cure, and you will still have to face the existential challenge of choosing life each moment of each day, it's also true that there is a lot of help available for people experiencing mental suffering of all kinds. Not every therapist is good. Not every drug is helpful. Not every treatment works. But we've learned a lot. There are trained, caring people who can help you. And when your friends and family encourage you to get professional psychiatric and psychological help, don't let your pride or fears stop you. Trust your loved ones, keep trying, and keep advocating for yourself.

For many of us, trusting our friends and medical professionals can be extraordinarily difficult when we are in a period of mental distress. Our suffering is so real and immediate and persuasive that the hope and confidence of our friends feels misplaced. It's hard to believe their words of comfort or advice. In learning to accept help and surrender control, I have found great comfort from this advice by Puritan theologian Richard Baxter:

> Do not trust your own judgment in your depressed and anxious condition, as to either the state of your soul or the choice and conduct of your thoughts or ways.

Commit yourself to the judgment and direction of some experienced, faithful guide. In this dark, disordered condition, you are unfit to judge your own condition or the way to approach your duty. . . . A wise person, when sick, will entrust himself, under God, to the direction of his physician and the help of his friends, and not resist their help and advice or willfully refuse it just because it doesn't please him. Do the same, if you are wise. Trust yourself to some appropriate advice. Don't despise the giver's judgment about either your condition or your duty. You think that you are lost and that there is no hope. Listen to someone in a better position to judge.[32]

Baxter's counsel is firmly worded but wise. For some of us, there will be times in our lives when we must accept that our judgment is distorted. We can't think clearly. When those periods come, our whole duty is to "commit [ourselves] to the judgment and direction of some experienced, faithful guide." I suspect that Protestants like myself (especially American Protestants, with our love of independence and self-reliance) will bristle at the idea of putting so much trust in an authority figure. Not everyone is worthy of that level of trust, but such people exist. Elders, pastors, counselors, psychologists, therapists, and so on. Baxter goes on to admonish the depressed and anxious Christian to "commit yourself to the care of your physician and obey him."[33] You don't cease to have duties while you are mentally sick, but your main duty is to trust in trustworthy men and women, especially professionals.

Regrettably, for too many people in our society, professional help is inaccessible or very difficult to access. Qualified therapists are costly. Medications can be costly, even the generic brands. When someone is poor and suffers from a mental illness, the monthly expense of medication can feel like a selfish luxury, even when it is precisely that medication that enables the person to hold a job. And in many places, qualified professionals are nowhere to be found. And qualified professionals make a difference. While a general practitioner can prescribe antidepressants, they cannot provide the level of care and expertise a psychiatrist can. I wish I could tell you that wherever you live and however much money you have, you can get the mental health care you need. But that isn't true.

It's not fair, but some people have much, much more difficult lives than you or me or most Americans. It is hard for almost anyone to accept that they need professional help, but it's especially hard when you can't find that help and can't afford it even if you could find it. We should all do what we can in our spheres of influence to increase access to quality mental health care. But until access is more universal, some of us will have to be stronger and bolder and more vulnerable. If you cannot afford the help you need, please ask for that help. Speak to friends and family. Talk to your church. If you cannot find the help you need locally, look into telemedicine—which is not as good as meeting in person but is far, far better than trying to fix everything on your own and getting lost in your head.

Although I highly recommend professional mental health services, I also think we have professionalized some of the basic life care that used to be done by mentors, parents and grandparents, older people in the church, elders, pastors, teachers, and other wise people. Our economy tends to commercialize and professionalize everything, including the most basic human interactions, such as mentorship, friendship, and discipleship. Many lesser instances of anxiety, distress, and depression could be alleviated with the loving counsel of a wise friend. We all need the loving counsel of a wise friend. Try to find one.

You should not be surprised if there are times in your life when you simply cannot trust your own reason, your feelings, your intuition, or the guilt gnawing at your gut and flooding your thoughts. What feels most real and certain about you and the world will be wrong, a lie conjured by your fallen mind or Satan or who knows what. It's awful, and I wish to

God no one had to experience this. Few things are more counterintuitive than choosing to accept that you can't trust your thoughts. But in these moments you have to trust people around you, which is what *con-science* means—to know *with* other people. That's scary, I know. If you let yourself, you can think of all kinds of reasons not to trust your friends or doctors or anyone at all. In your own experience and your knowledge of history and human nature, there is more than enough evidence to convince yourself that other people are untrustworthy and the only one you can trust is yourself.

But that's part of the lie. Because you actually do know for certain that your mind can deceive you and that there are wise, loving people in this world. Maybe the best you can do if you feel this way is to ask God to provide you with wise counselors, and then trust that God is faithful. He promises to give wisdom to *all* who ask (James 1:5). So trust that He will send you the people you need in order to see clearly. The alternative is a private "conscience," and that is a terrifying thought.

There sat down, once, a thing on Henry's heart
só heavy, if he had a hundred years
& more, & weeping, sleepless, in all them time
Henry could not make good.

JOHN BERRYMAN, "DREAM SONG 29"

ONE OF THE HARDEST TIMES to trust others is when you suffer from feelings of false guilt—when you wrongly imagine that you have committed some sin or when you reject God's pardon for your forgiven sins. The nature of false guilt is that you don't think it's false guilt, or at least you aren't *certain* it's false guilt. That uncertainty is a major source of suffering. Because you believe the lie of your guilt, when your friends assure you that you are forgiven or that your conscience is mistaken, you think they are untrustworthy or at least morally compromised. What's hard to see is that they are right and that you need to trust them.

To make matters worse, the more you come to understand the world and your own heart, the more you will discover how hard it is to live rightly. You can wound your neighbor by not saying good morning to them. You can lust in your heart before you know what's happening. You can excuse any sin, any evil, given enough time and the desire. Which means that if you really want to, you can feel guilty all the time. There's bound to be some way you're sinning, some way you're harming others, breaking the law, or dishonoring God. But that moral uncertainty also means that you can very easily imagine guilt where there is no true guilt.

I have often taken comfort from John's first epistle, where he writes, "For whenever our heart condemns us, God is greater than our heart, and he knows everything" (1 John 3:20). That last clause can be really terrifying if you think about it. When you experience false feelings of guilt, the very thing you are most afraid of is that God knows everything about you. He knows the sin you hide from the world and the sin you hide from yourself. And until you identify your hidden sin, repent, and make recompense, God will turn His face from you—that's the fear. It's not reality, but it is the fear. So how could anyone possibly find *comfort* in standing transparently before an almighty, all-knowing God? It might seem counter-intuitive, but only if you can be known absolutely, without deception or confusion, only then can you know when and where you are in sin.

If God were only all-knowing, His witness to our lives would be condemnation. But we know something more about God's character. We know that He desires our good. We know that He desires that none should perish (2 Peter 3:9). We know that He works all things together for the good of those who love Him (Romans 8:28). And we know that He gives wisdom to all who ask (James 1:5). All of this means that we can come before God whenever we experience guilt, and we can pray for discernment. We can pray that He would reveal where sin is in our lives and grant us peace from self-accusations. And we can trust that He will guide us. He sent His Holy Spirit just for this purpose. To help us and comfort us. He created His church, His body here on earth, to help us sort these things out. He *desires* us to know righteousness. God is not in the business of tricking people by hiding their sins from them.

So when your heart condemns you, remind yourself that your heart is not the judge of the universe. It's not even the judge of you. Only God sees you truly. And if you turn to Him for guidance, He will illuminate the areas where you truly are in sin, and He will give you peace for the guilt that you wrongly feel.

I may not know in every situation whether my feelings of guilt are convictions or irrational fears, but I know for certain a few things about God. He is greater than my heart and greater than my experience of dread. He knows me truly. He desires me to be righteous. And He will guide me with His Spirit. My task, as Francis Schaeffer describes it in *True Spirituality*, is to be faithful to the things above the surface—to what I know to be sin.[34]

But I know one more critical truth: because of Christ's finished work on the cross, because I am in union with Him, there is no condemnation for me. Even when I am in sin, I can reject the accusations of my flesh and the devil that crush my spirit and leave me in despair. I can throw myself before God, and He will forgive me and give me the grace to turn from sin. That process of turning may be painful, but it is always only a temporary burning away of dross. The deeper truth remains. The end of the story is written in eternity. I *have been* redeemed. So even when I must go through a period of discipline and repentance, God walks with me. And if I feel a sense of dread, existential guilt and shame, or the intrusive thought that I am damned or unworthy, I *know* that is a lie, even though I am still a sinner! Because Christ took on that condemnation for me.

This is one of the reasons it's so important to go to the Lord's Table regularly. For in that act of receiving God's means of grace, we *practice* God's forgiveness of us. Every time we eat the bread and drink the wine, we are sinners. In our hearts there remain lust, envy, pride, ingratitude toward God. And yet we are reminded that our justification is complete. We need this practice because without it I fear most of us would despair of ever being righteous. We commune with God because we are already righteous in His eyes because He sees the righteousness of His Son imputed to us. And by coming to the Table together, we remind one another that we are all fallen and yet righteous before God.

One of the most destructive ideas I was taught in the church as a young person was that if you *feel* like you are in sin, that must be your conscience convicting you. Or if you don't feel "at peace" with a decision or an action, that is the Holy Spirit telling you something. While I have no doubt that God does speak to us through His Spirit, I have also come to learn that just because you don't feel at peace, just because you feel guilty or uneasy or anxious, does not mean you are being spoken to by God. Sometimes you just feel bad. I wish someone had told me this sooner. You can even feel very, very bad—guilty and anxious and terrified. And it is on those days in particular when we need godly counselors to comfort us. By knowing together as the body of Christ, we can both exhort and comfort one another when we feel irrational guilt and shame.

∽

When you choose to trust the wisdom of others against your own intense thoughts, that trust doesn't usually change how you feel or what you think—at least not at first. But you're not responsible for spontaneously changing your thoughts. In fact, if you try to fight your mind when it has turned against you, you may spiral further into intense irrational thoughts. Reasoning with unreasonable people, even if *you* are the unreasonable person, is a fool's errand. It's a sand trap. Your task is not to *feel* right but to *act* right. Trusting the wisdom of others, accepting that the only true conscience is "knowing with" others, looks like *acting*. Like *doing* something. It has almost nothing to do with being convinced or feeling "peace." (How often I have felt "peace" when there was no peace and felt dread when I was perfectly safe!) It has everything to do with getting out of bed. Putting on your clothes. Eating breakfast. Doing the next good thing you need to do, however simple, however small. Taking a step to the block. Such are the tiny, mundane acts of faithfulness that make up our lives.

For nothing is real save his grace.

Cormac McCarthy, *The Crossing*

I N THE END, the only reason to keep living is if you live before God for His glory. If His Word is true, then we were divinely created to glorify Him and enjoy Him always. And our creation was a fundamentally *good* act—good and prodigal. Neither earned nor necessary but a gracious gift. And when we live in gratitude, recognizing and delighting in this life, we honor God.

The only other reasons to live are for the World, the Flesh, or the Devil, and they only care about you so long as you are *useful* to them.

Once you stop being productive and your credit dries up so that you can no longer consume and stimulate the economy, the World is utterly indifferent to your existence—unless, of course, that existence becomes a drain on the economy, in which case the World then views you as a threat. To the World, you are only useful while you contribute something to the grand project of living free from dependence on God (which has been humanity's mission since the beginning). And if you are not useful, your life does not matter.

Once your body experiences more pain than pleasure, your Flesh has no reason to keep going. When sex loses its thrill, and you've come to the end of porn, and all entertainment bores you; when your quality of life is diminished by mental illness or physical ailment; when you believe you'll always be alone; then assisted suicide seems reasonable and moral. To your Flesh, you are only useful while your personal experience of life is a net positive. And if you are not useful, your life is not worth enduring.

To "live for the Devil" may sound like a paranoid superstition or the title of a bad heavy metal album, but it has a very real and very terrible reality. If living before God means that we accept that His acts of creation and preservation are good, and we give our assent to His sovereignty and goodness by living with gratitude in His world, then to live for the Devil is to deny God's sovereignty and goodness, or the goodness of His creation and preservation of us. You may do this by willfully destroying your life (slowly through dissipation or quickly), or encouraging others to destroy their lives, or actively destroying the lives of others through exploitation and violence. All of these actions defy God and His goodness by treating what is precious as worthless and treating what is a gift as a curse. A great many people devote their lives to hopelessness because even in despair you may be entertained and find pleasure in your misery. But you can also defy God by insisting on your own self-sufficiency. If you can achieve enough success and be a self-made person, the author of your own story and the definer of your own identity, then what use have you for God? In this way, a great many people devote their lives to mastering themselves and everyone around them. Whether you live for the Devil by destroying what God has made good or by denying your dependence on God, your value is determined by the effectiveness of your rebellion.

Usefulness is the sole criterion for the World, the Flesh, or the Devil. But you have no *use value* to God. You can't. There is nothing He needs. You can't cease being useful to God because you were never useful to begin with. That's not why He created you, and it's not why He continues to sustain your existence in the world. His creation of you was gratuitous, prodigal. He made you just because He loves you and for His own good pleasure. Every other reason to live demands that you remain useful, and one day your use will run out.

If you live for the World, the Flesh, or the Devil, there is no room for grace, or for God's gifts. But to God, your existence in His universe is a good act of creation, and it remains good *as* God's creation, even in its fallen state.

~

We all suffer silent crises, carrying burdens that are incommunicable to those closest to us and occasionally even opaque to ourselves. Some suffer from diagnosed mental illnesses, some from undiagnosed, and some from mental suffering that has no medical categorization yet is no less real and terrible and hard. But your existence is good.

Even when you can't feel it or rationally understand it, life remains good. And while suffering is a normal part of fallen human life, it is not the essence of life. At the center of existence is not suffering but grace—the grace of Christ. The grace that created you, that cleanses you from all unrighteousness and provides all the blessings of this life. The same God who sent His Son to die for you sustains your existence and created you—*you*—miraculous you, because He loves you. Whether you believe it or not.

At the heart of being is grace, not suffering. "For nothing is real save his grace."[35] We will forget this fact many times throughout our lives. The task before us is to hold each other up, to remind one another of the truth that is truer than our deepest misery, to attend to the gift God has given us, and to accept that our lives are good even when we do not feel that goodness at all.

One of the most comforting verses in all of the Bible is Philippians 4:6-7, when Paul commands us to not be anxious for anything (good luck with that one) but to pray and let our requests be made known to God. Paul tells us that when we do this—when we stop trying to internalize all our anxiety or fix everything ourselves, but we turn to God, acknowledging our dependence on Him and giving thanks—then "the peace of God, which surpasses all understanding, will guard your hearts and your minds in Christ Jesus."

These verses have sometimes been twisted to claim that all anxiety is merely a failure to trust God. And while sometimes that *is* why we are anxious, it is not the only reason. What Paul offers is not an alternative to therapy and medication nor a simple fix to the agony that often abides. Instead, he offers us a peace that can enable us to carry on.

What gets me every time is that the peace of God goes beyond "all understanding." I don't know how I would handle life if this weren't true. Very often, I cannot understand how I can have any peace or how I could deserve any peace. I cannot rationally see that things are okay, or that they ever could be okay. I don't understand how *I* could be okay. I can't solve things or see a way out of the messes I'm in. Sometimes I cannot even imagine tomorrow, or at least a tomorrow worth getting out of bed for.

But none of that matters. God's peace is in no way constrained by my imagination. I don't have to have a rational explanation for why my suffering is worth enduring today—and that's not what I need anyway. I need both my heart and my mind to be comforted, to be guarded. My emotions and my thoughts will betray me, but I know He is faithful.

Meditating on these verses usually does not jar me out of my anxiety. But it does ground me. It reminds me why I can persevere. I may only be able to say, "Lord, I do not feel nor understand Your peace, but I know Your peace is beyond my understanding. So I will trust You. And I will act."

At the end of *The Road*, the father must take a leap of faith. Because he is dying, he had planned to kill his son to protect him from greater suffering after he himself is gone. But when the time comes, he chooses instead to let his son live, trusting in the goodness of God—that God will care for his son despite the horrific dangers of the world. The father's peace is an uneasy peace, and it comes at great personal cost.

Sometimes that's what peace is: an action based on faith and not an emotional state. The father in the novel has peace because he trusts in God beyond all his own understanding. Some days that may be all you have: the knowledge that God loves you and desires you to get out of bed, regardless of all the reasons you may find to give up. So you act out your peace in fear and trembling.

~

Despite the comforts of contemporary life and its promises of even greater peace and self-mastery, life is terribly hard. A comfortable, pleasant life isn't normal. And while we may hesitate to call getting out of bed "courageous," it is undeniably true that day-to-day life demands a great deal of courage.

And that courage speaks loudly. It shouts. It confesses the nature of creation and of God. It is our burden and our gift. It is our spiritual act of worship, presenting our body as a living sacrifice. You have no idea how many people are strengthened by your courage. You have no way of knowing the influence your faithfulness and long-suffering have on loved ones, neighbors, strangers, and even people who will live generations after you.

None of this makes the duty of living easier, but it does remind us that our lives are never, ever only our own. We belong to God, and so we also belong to those around us, whether we know them or not.

And if you happen to be in a time of relative peace, don't be surprised if you slip back into a period of darkness when you can only move out by faithfully crawling inch by inch. The remarkable thing is that the dread you feel will be as unimaginable to you in the future as joy feels today.[36]

Your task is to be faithful: to do the next thing. And when you cannot get up on your own, let someone carry you, knowing that in due time you will be called on to do the same for others. And when you are blessed with the responsibility of carrying someone else, then your own experience with suffering, your own experience of depending on others, will give you the wisdom and empathy you need to love them well. Christ's body here on Earth is one of His greatest mercies to us. It's the only way we make it through.

One morning I lay in bed for hours, praying to have the strength to get up yet unable to move. And I heard a faint knock on my door. It was my seven-year-old daughter, who handed me a card she had made and said simply, "I hope you feel better, Daddy." That morning, she carried me out of bed, downstairs, and into life.

We all bear witness to the goodness of this existence God has given us. That witness has the power to move mountains, and to move broken forty-year-old men out of bed. And it's beautiful; even while we suffer, it's beautiful.

Because it's grace. Dear God, it's Your grace.

ACKNOWLEDGMENTS

MUCH OF THE WISDOM of this book has come from conversations, encouragement, and experiences with people I love and who have loved and suffered with me. I'm grateful for the love and support of my parents, Craig and Brenda. For the patience, encouragement, and love of my family: Brittany, Eleanor, Quentin, and Frances. For the friendship of Jonathan Callis, Shaynor Newsome, and Matt Wiley. For my students, who have taught me a lot about what it means to suffer. For Aaron New, Shaynor Newsome, and Elia Tyson for reading an early draft of this essay.

This book began as two essays: "On Living," published on my own Medium page, and "When Existence Becomes Seemingly Impossible," published at Christ and Pop Culture.[37] This book would not exist except for the support and encouragement I received from readers of these articles.

NOTES

[1] Anne Harrington, *Mind Fixers: Psychiatry's Troubled Search for the Biology of Mental Illness* (New York: W. W. Norton and Company, 2019), 273-74.

[2] Harrington, *Mind Fixers*, 272-73.

[3] Jacques Ellul, *The Technological Society*, trans. John Wilkinson (New York: Vintage Books, 1964), xxv.

[4] Alan Noble, *You Are Not Your Own* (Downers Grove, IL: InterVarsity Press, 2021).

[5] Franz Kafka, *The Metamorphosis*, trans. and ed. Stanley Corngold (New York: Bantam Books, 1972), 3.

[6] Cormac McCarthy, *The Road* (New York: Vintage Books, 2006), 114.

[7] Virgil, *Aeneid*, trans. Stanley Lombardo (Indianapolis: Hackett Publishing, 2005), 6.880.

[8] For one discussion of this mystery, see Jillian Mock, "How Antidepressants Work Is a Mystery Scientists Still Don't Understand," *Discover* magazine, July 22, 2020, www.discovermagazine.com/health/how-antidepressants-work-is-a-mystery-scientists-still-dont-understand.

[9] See Alain Ehrenberg, *The Weariness of Self: Diagnosing the History of Depression in the Contemporary Age* (Montreal: McGill-Queen's

University Press, 2010); and Jonathan Sadowsky, *The Empire of Depression: A New History* (Cambridge: Polity Press, 2021), 93-97.

[10] Sadowsky, *Empire of Depression*, 95.

[11] For more on the debate surrounding the removal of the bereavement exclusion, see Michael G. Kavan and Eugene J. Barone, "Grief and Major Depression—Controversy Over Changes in DSM-5 Diagnostic Criteria," *American Family Physician* 90, no. 10 (November 15, 2014), www.aafp.org/pubs/afp/issues/2014/1115/p690.html.

[12] William Shakespeare, *Hamlet*, ed. Barbara Mowat et al., The Folger Shakespeare Library, 3.1.66, https://shakespeare.folger.edu/shakespeares-works/hamlet/act-3-scene-1/.

[13] Pedro the Lion, "Priests and Paramedics," by David Bazan and Casey Foubert, *Control*, Jade Tree, 2002.

[14] McCarthy, *The Road*, 58.

[15] McCarthy, *The Road*, 5.

[16] McCarthy, *The Road*, 77.

[17] McCarthy, *The Road*, 137.

[18] McCarthy, *The Road*, 56.

[19] McCarthy, *The Road*, 269.

[20] McCarthy, *The Road*, 272.

[21] T. S. Eliot, "Little Gidding," from *Four Quartets* in *Collected Poems (1909–1962)* (London: Harcourt, 1991), 208.

[22] I originally came across this phrase, "do the next thing," in F. Scott Fitzgerald's *This Side of Paradise* (New York: Penguin Books, 1996), 96.

[23] Josef Pieper, *Faith, Hope, Love* (San Francisco: Ignatius Press, 2012), 174.

[24] J. D. Salinger, *Franny and Zooey* (Boston: Little, Brown and Company, 1961), 152.

25 O. Alan Noble (@TheAlanNoble), "With few exceptions: It doesn't get easier," Twitter, May 24, 2019, https://twitter.com/TheAlanNoble /status/1132070749806706688.

26 O. Alan Noble (@TheAlanNoble), "Do not mock His grace by rejecting it," Twitter, January 17, 2020, https://twitter.com/TheAlanNoble /status/1218196607075831810.

27 Pedro the Lion, "Priests and Paramedics."

28 Robert Lowell, "Home After Three Months Away," in *Life Studies and For the Union Dead* (New York: Farrar, Straus and Giroux, 2007), 88.

29 T. S. Eliot, "The Dry Salvages," from *Four Quartets*, 195.

30 Ralph Waldo Emerson, *The Essential Writings of Ralph Waldo Emerson* (New York: Random House Publishing Group, 2000), 309.

31 Emerson, *The Essential Writings of Ralph Waldo Emerson*, 309.

32 Michael S. Lundy and J. I. Packer, *Depression, Anxiety, and the Christian Life: Practical Wisdom from Richard Baxter* (Wheaton, IL: Crossway, 2018), 99-100.

33 Lundy and Packer, *Depression, Anxiety, and the Christian Life*, 100.

34 Francis Schaeffer, *True Spirituality*, in *The Complete Works of Francis A. Schaeffer: A Christian Worldview*, vol. 3, *A Christian View of Spirituality* (Wheaton, IL: Crossway Books, 1982), 324.

35 Cormac McCarthy, *The Crossing* (New York: Vintage Books, 1995), 158.

36 O. Alan Noble (@TheAlanNoble), "Do not be surprised when," Twitter, June 13, 2019, https://twitter.com/TheAlanNoble /status/1139246044632498177.

37 Alan Noble, "On Living," Medium, October 28, 2019, https:// thealannoble.medium.com/on-living-3363ce5bb6ac; and Alan Noble, "When Existence Becomes Seemingly Impossible," Christ and Pop Culture, August 13, 2014, https://christandpopculture.com /existence-becomes-seemingly-impossible/.

ALSO BY ALAN NOBLE

Disruptive Witness
978-0-8308-4483-8

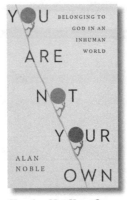

You Are Not Your Own
978-0-8308-4782-2